MILITARY ROLLS OF THE OUTWARD COMMONS

Soldiers of Wilbraham, Massachusetts

1730–1840

by J. Bruce Tingle

HERITAGE BOOKS
2012

HERITAGE BOOKS
AN IMPRINT OF HERITAGE BOOKS, INC.

Books, CDs, and more—Worldwide

For our listing of thousands of titles see our website
at
www.HeritageBooks.com

Published 2012 by
HERITAGE BOOKS, INC.
Publishing Division
100 Railroad Ave. #104
Westminster, Maryland 21157

International Standard Book Numbers
Paperbound: 978-0-7884-1541-8
Clothbound: 978-0-7884-9371-3

Dedication

This book is dedicated to my lovely wife Paula and our dear daughter Jessica. Thank you for continuing to inspire me.

- On the Cover -

The cover picture shows the Wilbraham United Church on Main Street in Wilbraham. This lovely picture is by Delight Rothery, a member of the church and one of the finest artists in Wilbraham.

The Wilbraham United Church's roots go back to the Congregational church in Wilbraham with Reverend Noah Merrick as its first minister in 1741. In the early 1790s, Charles Brewer and twelve others withdrew from the Congregational church and formed the First Methodist Society of Wilbraham. Following a fire that destroyed the Congregationalist church in 1911, the Methodists and Congregationalists met together in the Methodist church until the church was rebuilt in 1913. At that time they decided to continue to worship together. Today's Wilbraham United Church is the result of this confederation of the two churches.

Under the present leadership of Reverend Rob Stuart, Ph.D. and Reverend Lynne Dolan, the Wilbraham United Church continues to support the people of Wilbraham and the surrounding area.

- Table of Contents -

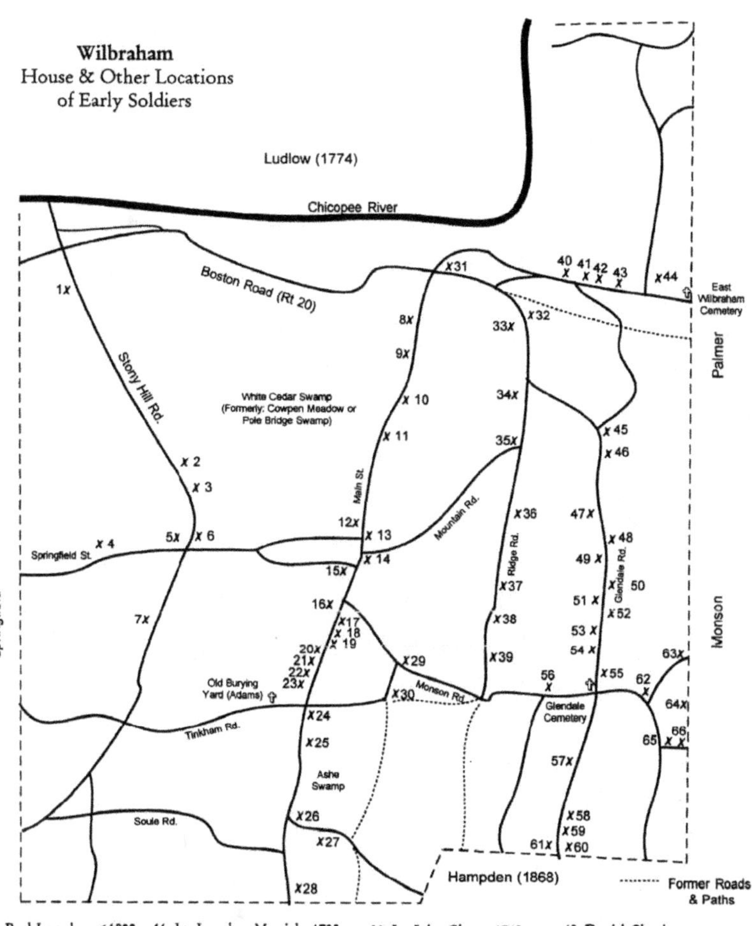

1. Capt. Paul Langdon <1800
2. Lt. Ephraim Fuller
3. Ezra Barker
4. David Jones 1770
5. Gaius Brewer
6. Benoni Atchinson 1745
7. Samuel Warner
8. Lorenzo Bliss
9. Levi Bliss 1772
10. Lt. Thomas Jones
11. Abel Bliss, Jr. <1814
12. Samuel Warner 1754
    Sgt. Daniel Cadwell 1765
    Eleaser Smith 1770
13. John Stearns 1768
14. Charles Brewer 1781
15. Isaac Brewer 1748
16. Lt. Jonathan Merrick 1735
17. Phineas Newton, Jr. /
    Joseph Sexton
18. Capt. Gideon Kibbe 1810
19. Maj. William Clark
20. Nathaniel Warriner
21. Nathaniel Hitchcock 1731 /
    Samuel F. Merrick
22. Solomon Warriner
23. Moses Burt
24. Chilea B. Merrick
25. Moses Warriner 1744
26. Philip Lyon 1768
27. Samuel Stebbins
28. Thomas Mirick 1734
29. Gideon Burt 1770
30. First Church 1744
31. Lt. John Glover 1742
32. Ens. Abel Bliss
33. Ens. Abel Bliss 1736
34. Capt. James Shaw
35. Moses Bartlett 1741
36. Judah Ely
37. Daniel Cadwell 1742
38. David Chapin 1740
39. Capt. Daniel Knowlton
40. Benjamin Butler
41. Jason Burt (CW?)
42. James Burt (CW?)
43. Seth Knowlton (??)
44. Baptist Church 1749
45. Royal Rindge (??)
46. John Rindge (??)
47. Almon Lard
48. Daniel Chapin
49. Stephen Cadwell
50. Nathaniel Knowlton
51. Calbe Stebbins 1744
52. Cyrus Edson (??)
53. Isaac Chapin
54. Samuel Bishop 1777
55. Deuty Partridge
56. Elijah Parsons 1768
57. Moses Hancock
58. Capt. Washman (??)
59. Shadrach Thayer (??)
60. Judah Willey 1763
61. Capt. John Carpenter
62. Moses Hancock
63. Ezra Knowlton (??)
64. Elijah Munsell (CW?)
65. George Mixter (CW?)
66. Seth Knowlton (??)

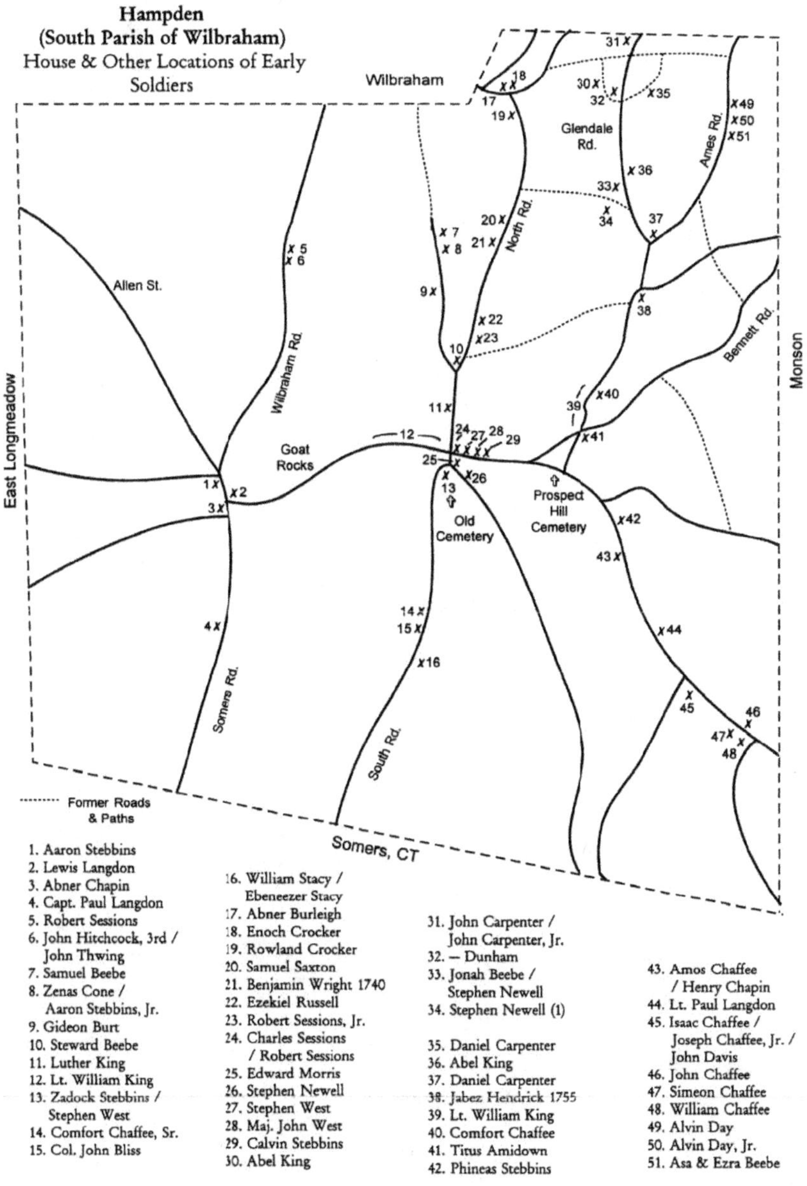
Hampden
(South Parish of Wilbraham)
House & Other Locations of Early Soldiers
Wilbraham
East Longmeadow
Monson
Somers, CT
Allen St.
Wilbraham Rd.
North Rd.
Glendale Rd.
Ames Rd.
Bennett Rd.
Somers Rd.
South Rd.
Goat Rocks
Old Cemetery
Prospect Hill Cemetery
Former Roads & Paths
1. Aaron Stebbins
2. Lewis Langdon
3. Abner Chapin
4. Capt. Paul Langdon
5. Robert Sessions
6. John Hitchcock, 3rd / John Thwing
7. Samuel Beebe
8. Zenas Cone / Aaron Stebbins, Jr.
9. Gideon Burt
10. Steward Beebe
11. Luther King
12. Lt. William King
13. Zadock Stebbins / Stephen West
14. Comfort Chaffee, Sr.
15. Col. John Bliss
16. William Stacy / Ebeneezer Stacy
17. Abner Burleigh
18. Enoch Crocker
19. Rowland Crocker
20. Samuel Saxton
21. Benjamin Wright 1740
22. Ezekiel Russell
23. Robert Sessions, Jr.
24. Charles Sessions / Robert Sessions
25. Edward Morris
26. Stephen Newell
27. Stephen West
28. Maj. John West
29. Calvin Stebbins
30. Abel King
31. John Carpenter / John Carpenter, Jr.
32. – Dunham
33. Jonah Beebe / Stephen Newell
34. Stephen Newell (1)
35. Daniel Carpenter
36. Abel King
37. Daniel Carpenter
38. Jabez Hendrick 1755
39. Lt. William King
40. Comfort Chaffee
41. Titus Amidown
42. Phineas Stebbins
43. Amos Chaffee / Henry Chapin
44. Lt. Paul Langdon
45. Isaac Chaffee / Joseph Chaffee, Jr. / John Davis
46. John Chaffee
47. Simeon Chaffee
48. William Chaffee
49. Alvin Day
50. Alvin Day, Jr.
51. Asa & Ezra Beebe

I. Overview

General

Don't look for "George Washington Slept Here" signs in Wilbraham. Our sign would most accurately read "The American War for Independence - Nothing Happened Here" (with the exception of a few historical figures passing through on their way somewhere else, most notably General Knox and General Burgoyne).

On the other hand, the call to arms was answered in Wilbraham by a substantial number of men. While you don't see their names in history books, many of them, nonetheless, contributed greatly to the struggles and to our own local history.

The trail that led to this work started when I looked at several different lists of veterans buried in Wilbraham cemeteries. Based on the very few names listed, my hunch was that these lists were quite incomplete. I then spent time with the 1863 Stebbins, 1903 Peck, and 1963 Merrick Wilbraham Town histories. Although these volumes had more information, they still did not provide all the information I felt was available. If nothing else, I wanted more information about the particular struggles our men endured and wanted to know whatever I could discover about the men themselves.

I have subsequently spent whatever time I could looking at various history books and documents to try to fill in some of the missing pieces. In addition, I have walked our town cemeteries and other local cemeteries to record what information is available on the gravestones. During these walks, I have identified several names of veterans of the early period who, while not identified in the Wilbraham histories, nonetheless ended up in the Wilbraham and Hampden "burying grounds" and who should be included here. For example, Nathan Barker rests in East Wilbraham. On his gravestone are the words "a soldier of the revolution." While Mr. Barker did not belong to Wilbraham's militia, I was able to validate his service in the Revolution and I am including him in this document.

Including people, such as Mr. Barker, is appropriate as, no matter where his home was once, his final home is Wilbraham and his service as a veteran should be remembered.

This work then attempts to provide a more complete listing of early Wilbraham soldiers and the other roles many of them played. While it relies heavily on the Stebbins, Peck, and Merrick histories, it also contains material gathered from onsite walks through town and other local cemeteries, old history books, and the World Wide Web. Arguably, this work might not be complete and, perhaps, updated versions will be produced as more information is brought to light. For now at least, it is appropriate to produce version one and bring closure to the initial research.

Disclaimers

I am only an amateur in the world of research. I have gone through many books and documents in my search. Unfortunately, I did not make note of every source as I compiled my lists. While I have included a list of the major references I used, if I hurt anyone's feelings for not doing a fully footnoted professional document, I apologize. It is also possible that I have made a mistake or two. If so, again, I apologize.

Families

One of the first observations I made about the early period of Wilbraham military history was to note the heavy involvement of several families who are not well represented in town today. Certainly, the vagaries of timing played a role in this. That is, some families at this time period were large already and had several sons at the right age to be involved. This is not to say families with fewer sons didn't contribute, only that some family names seem to show up more often. As an example, according to the 1903 Peck History, nine Chaffees (fathers and sons) answered the militia call for Shay's Rebellion in 1789.

The 1863 Stebbins history also supports this observation. In Mr. Stebbins' genealogy section (page 292) he wrote: "The Colton's are nearly all gone. So of the Joneses and Ely's. The Shaw's, and Glovers, and Bartletts are all gone I believe.

Nathaniel Bliss's family are all gone; so of the Lyons, and Carpenters, and Woods, and Skinners, and Badgers. Of the thirteen [!] families of Stebbins, once in the South Parish [Hampden], there is but one family left."

The period from the Revolution through the Civil War was a time of the great migration westward. Some of our early families moved west, or to other towns, or just died out. The more recent names in Stebbins' genealogy, in fact, tend to reflect this movement of even the remaining families, with the grandchildren and great-grandchildren showing up in Ohio, Louisiana, etc. as well as in many neighboring New England states.

The Town's Beginning

All the land to the east of Springfield, which was founded in 1636, was commonly owned, and known as the "Outward Commons". It was little used by the inhabitants of the town except for foraging for wood and berries and hunting. To forestall a threatened revocation of the charter for the commons by the Governor, a town meeting on February 3rd, 1685, voted to assign these Outward Commons to a group of 125 proprietors. These proprietors were each of the 122 heads of families in Springfield plus the "reverend teacher" (the minister), and the local school. Each parcel of land was to extend to the eastern boundary of the town, some four miles away.

No actual survey was made of the lots until 1729, but by 1727, Nathaniel Hitchcock had acquired title to sufficient land for his purposes. In the summer of 1730, he came out to his tract and built a log hut (near the present Bennett Turkey Farm on Main Street). The next spring, in 1731, he came back with his wife and baby to live on his farm; thus the Hitchcocks were the first white settlers of Wilbraham.

For a whole year the Hitchcocks lived alone. In the spring of 1732, Noah Alvord settled just south of them, and the next year Daniel Warner arrived. Nathaniel Warriner was the next settler. He came the following year. Settlement was still slow and at the end of ten years there were only twenty-five families living in the community. They set up a school with funds appropriated by Springfield for a school in the Outward Commons.

The Outward Commons had become sufficiently populated to support a church of its own, and in 1740 the men of the community petitioned the General Court to allow them to become a separate precinct, or parish, and build a church. The petition was granted on January 6, 1741, and the Outward Commons became the Fourth Precinct of Springfield. Precinct officers were elected at a meeting on March 12, 1741, and on June 24, 1741, the Reverend Noah Merrick was ordained pastor of the church.

In 1740, a precinct and a parish were one and the same, and the affairs of one were the affairs of the other. For several years, the chief problems of the precinct were church problems: building a house for the minister, locating and constructing a meetinghouse, and settling the question of the minister's salary. It was becoming obvious that a community so far from Springfield would gradually feel itself a separate unit with its own local problems and be less and less concerned with those of the larger town.

From 1749 on, various attempts were made to get Springfield to set them off as a "district", but efforts were not successful. Finally in 1763, after an appeal to the General Court, Springfield gave in, and on June 15th of that year Wilbraham became a separate town.

Criteria for Inclusion in this Book

The previous town “histories” were not necessarily inaccurate as much as they were incomplete. For this work, I have researched every source I could to identify and list “Wilbraham” soldiers. While the following criteria is specifically for the Revolutionary War, the same general criteria was used for all of the sections of this book.

1. Identifiable as living in Wilbraham (and Hampden) during the war. Where possible, I have indicated in the list that the soldier lived in Hampden. All records of the

Commonwealth give residences as Wilbraham since, at the time, Hampden did not exist as a separate entity. It is almost certain that many of the men identified as being "Wilbraham" residents actually lived in what is now Hampden. This is especially true of families such as the Chaffees and Stebbins.

2. Identifiable as having enlisted for Wilbraham, even though residence was in another town.
3. Of unknown residence, but served at one time under one of Wilbraham's Captains. The exception to this is someone not from Wilbraham, or whose residence is not identifiable, who served in Captain John Carpenter's Guards. The Guards unit was not a function of the Wilbraham Militia units. Only those men from Wilbraham are listed in my "Guards" list.
4. Buried in one of the Wilbraham or Hampden cemeteries. Even if they did not serve in a "Wilbraham" unit, the fact that they are buried here makes them part of our heritage.

Sources, References, etc.

The starting point for this research was the 1863 town history (*Historical Address*) by Rev. Rufus Stebbins. The later versions by Chauncey Peck (1903) and Charles Merrick (1963) add to the Stebbins lists but the military rolls are still quite incomplete.

The primary reference for this work was the *Massachusetts Revolutionary War Soldiers and Sailors 1775 – 1782*. This enormous work, seventeen volumes with 175,000 records, was ordered by the General Court in 1891. Generally an index of the names of those that served in the Revolution, it was developed by compiling the names of those who appeared on any muster roll, order, receipt, etc. that could be found in the archives of the Commonwealth. However, it does not necessarily contain the name of everyone who served nor does it necessarily reflect the actual service of everyone listed. Until 1840, the militia was a local responsibility. Accordingly, records from the Revolution were stored in the various town halls with various storage techniques employed. In 1840, when the State assumed control of the militia, some of the towns destroyed much of the local material, as there was no longer any requirement for them to store it. The result of this was that some of the types of records that were used to compile the *Massachusetts Soldiers and Sailors* were destroyed years before it was decided to compile a complete record.

The preface of the *Massachusetts Soldiers and Sailors* also makes mention that the rolls of the Lexington Alarm of April 20, 1775, is the most complete and accurate of all of the events of the Revolution. The year 1776, on the other hand, is the most inaccurate and incomplete due to the turmoil of that year.

If a soldier's name, for whatever reason, did not appear on a piece of paper in the archives, his name will not be found in this work. Additionally, no effort was made to "force residence" on anyone. If a list contained the name "John Jones," he was entered as "John Jones" with no attempt made to combine his service with "John Jones of Springfield," even though they were the same individual. I have attempted to do this whenever it was obvious, but I have done so in a conservative manner.

Another factor to bear in mind relative to records of this period is that spelling was not really a strong suite of the record keepers. Depending on who wrote down the information, a name might be spelled any number of different ways. We have in our town, for example, Merrick, Mirick, Mirrick, Myrick, etc. along with Lillie, Lillee, Lilley, etc.

Also complicating matters was the fashion of the time to repeat common given names throughout the various branches of a family. This would result, for example, in their being several "Joshua's" in a family, all of whom were about the same age. Based on the information contained in the State records, there is no way to discern which Joshua actually engaged in any specific military affair. In our own case, there are Nathaniel Hitchcock's in Wilbraham, Westfield, and Springfield, all of whom appear to be the same man.

One final factor that complicates matters is the time of service allowed for a soldier. It was a common practice to allow an additional day of service for each twenty miles of travel required for the soldier to go to or return from his assigned post. In the State records, therefore, one will often see the terms "time allowed" and "actual service." In the case of the Bennington Alarm for Captain Shaw's men, the total service is 32 days, while actual service (total minus 8 days travel time allowed) is 24 days.

The *Massachusetts Soldiers and Sailors,* therefore, is a valuable resource for the researcher, but it does not, by itself, prove service in the Revolution. In the listing contained within this book of Wilbraham military men, the phrase "No State records" should be taken to mean I was unable to find an individual in the *Massachusetts Soldiers and Sailors.*

Accuracy

This work is more accurate (although undoubtedly not perfect) than previous works of its type. Primarily this is because of the technology now available. The *Massachusetts Soldiers and Sailors,* for example, is available on both compact disc (CD-ROM) and on the Internet and can easily be searched electronically.

I also had electronic access to over 150 volumes of the Daughters of the American Revolution (D.A.R.) Lineage books. These books have over 1.85 million names and trace ancestry back to a Revolutionary War soldier. Unfortunately, some of the information in the D.A.R. books is of dubious accuracy and I had to spend quite a lot of time attempting to verify it.

Along with the *Massachusetts Soldiers and Sailors* and D.A.R. Lineage books, there were quite a few Internet sites with bits and pieces of information about our soldiers or the conflict itself. Using a computer to search for all the references to the word "Wilbraham" is much easier than manually flipping and scanning pages in a traditional paper book.

Lastly, the good, old-fashioned library provided a wealth of information. Both the Wilbraham Library Historical Collection and the archives at the Connecticut Valley Historical Museum provided significant information. My feet also played a role as they carried me through almost every area cemetery searching for information on gravestones.

It is not surprising that this list of soldiers should be more complete and contain more detail than previous works. What is surprising to me is how accurate the previous works are, given the limited and cumbersome resources available in past years. We should appreciate the work done by Mr. Stebbins, Mr. Peck, and Mr. Merrick.

II. THE COLONIAL PERIOD

Background

The Tudors revived the English militia in the sixteenth century as a way of avoiding the expense of a large standing army. They instituted the traditional universal obligation of defending the realm as the basis for forming and maintaining voluntary "trained bands."

The early settlements in Virginia, Massachusetts and Connecticut recruited professional soldiers as military advisers but utilized the English militia tradition to form militia units to protect their settlements. Massachusetts became the first colony to establish permanent regiments in 1636. In fact, standing regiments didn't appear in the English Army itself until the 1640's.

The origin of the Western Massachusetts militia units goes back to November 14, 1639 when the Springfield Train Band was mustered into service to defend this area from attacks by Indians. The Train Band was reorganized on May 31, 1671 and officially became the Hampshire Regiment. John Pynchon was the Sergeant Major. A Sergeant Major then was a commissioned officer and is not the same as today's sergeant major, an enlisted man. The regiment participated in many of the conflicts in the early days, including Queen Anne's War (1702 - 1713), King George's War (1744 - 1748), and the French and Indian War (1753 - 1760). It is in the latter two wars that we first see men from Wilbraham identified as participants. Prior to this period, the men were all considered to be part of the Springfield unit.

Until the summer of 1745, all men (except Rev. Noah Merrick) were listed in the South Company of Springfield, part of the Hampshire Regiment. The regiment was reorganized in 1748 into the North and South Hampshire regiments. In the muster of March 1749, the Wilbraham Company became the 4th Springfield Company (East Company) for the Outward Commons. Lt. Samuel Day and Ensign Thomas Merrick of Wilbraham were officers in this company. The regiment was again reorganized in 1763 when the Berkshire regiment was added.

Military service for all males between the ages of 16 and 60 had been obligatory in the Bay Colony since 1631. Children between the ages of 10 and 16 were also allowed to train with the militia with their parent's permission. Their fellow townsmen elected officers. Only freemen, those with full citizenship, could be officers.

Interestingly, The Massachusetts General Laws (ch 33, sec 2 Militia Organization) still state that:

"The militia of the commonwealth shall consist of all able-bodied male citizens and all other able-bodied males who have declared their intention to become citizens of the United States, between the ages of seventeen and forty-five, and who are residents of the commonwealth, and of such other persons, male and female, as may, upon their own application, be enlisted or commissioned therein pursuant to any provision of this chapter, subject, however, to such exemptions as are now, or may be hereafter, created by law."

Whether this is intended to allow hordes of untrained accountants, lawyers, and other hearty types to defend our borders against unruly tourists is unclear but it is probably no more harmful than most laws.

Obviously fulfilling the age requirements of the law, at the July 1754 muster Samuel Day was 56, Thomas Merrick was 51, and Abel Bliss was 46.

For the 1755-1759 period, Mr. Stebbins' research was limited, by his own admission, as he only had access to a list of soldiers from the Fourth Precinct of Springfield. Our men belonged to that precinct for military purposes. He used a church roll from 1760 to determine whether a Wilbraham man was listed in the military. Some additional effort was made through the military rolls in the Secretary of State's office but Mr. Stebbins indicated he was not too successful at that venture due to the way the rolls were ordered. The men were listed under the colonel and captain of the company in which they served rather than alphabetically. While Mr. Stebbins did the best job he could, given the materials available, the list of soldiers he identified in his 1863 history is incomplete.

King George's War

The French, who controlled most of Canada, the Ohio Valley westward, and Louisiana, objected to the westward and northward expansion of the English colonies. The English at Oswego, New York, in particular were very successful at trading with the Indians for furs, at the expense of the French. To seal off the north, the French moved to establish a firm line along their boundaries.

The war began on March 20th, 1744 and ended on October 7th, 1748 with the treaty of Aix-la-Chapelle. In this conflict, the French stronghold, Louisburg, at Cape Breton was ordered captured by Governor Shirley of Massachusetts. France had spent millions on this fort and with its walls of solid masonry thirty feet thick, believed it to be impregnable. But with the help of the British fleet, Colonel Pepperrell of Maine with his few thousand Yankee farmers and fishermen rather easily took

Fortress Louisburg

the fort on June 16th, 1744. Still, nervous about losing it back to France, the British established Halifax on the southern end of Cape Breton to guard the approaches to the fort and to protect British shipping in New England.

Of notable interest to Western Massachusetts was the line of forts built along our western boundaries beginning in 1744 to defend against French incursions. Four forts were built - one at Blandford, Fort Pelham at Rowe, Fort Shirley at Heath, and

Fort Massachusetts at Adams. Several Wilbraham men were involved in the construction of Fort Massachusetts (see later in this section). These forts were under the immediate supervision of Captain Ephraim Williams. Captain Williams would later gain notoriety in the French and Indian War at Lake George as a colonel.

On August 26, 1746, a force of 800-900 French and Indians attacked Fort Massachusetts. The 22-man garrison held out for 28 hours but then surrendered. Raids were also made by a small number of this force on Deerfield where three colonists were killed and a young boy was taken prisoner.

In 1748 on August 2nd, a force of about 200 Indians again attacked Fort Massachusetts. Garrisoned at that time by about a hundred men under Captain Williams, the attack was beaten off.

The French and Indian War

The French and Indian War began in 1754 and ended in 1763. The major "movements in the field" went on during the 1755 to 1759 time period. The question that had yet to be answered in the previous conflicts between France and Great Britain was whether the French or English would control North America. Although the English population far outnumbered the French, France had possession of the St. Lawrence and Mississippi Rivers. The French had also built a line of forts down these rivers from Quebec all the way to the Gulf of Mexico.

England continued to try to expand its trading to the north and west. This, of course, did not fill the French with joy and one of the major aims of the French in the beginning of the war was to remove Oswego as an English trading center. Along with this, they planned to move aggressively down Lake Champlain and Lake George to halt further expansion by Great Britain. At that time, Albany was the northern outpost to protect settlers against Canadian war parties. France preferred to keep it that way.

Of primary interest to Wilbraham is the Battle of Lake

George in 1755 and the second expedition to Crown Point in 1759.

The Battle of Lake George

The French-built Fort St. Frederic, built in 1731 at Crown Point, posed a major threat to British installations at Ticonderoga. Eagerly supported by Massachusetts who had 4,500 volunteers (1 in 8 adult males), Sir William Johnson of New York was chosen to lead the expedition to placate the other states. He was designated a Major General by all the states for this campaign

Johnson had Fort St. Frederic as his objective when he left Albany in August of 1755 and had a military road built from Fort Edward (originally Fort Lyman) to the head of what is now Lake George. Hearing of this plan, the French Baron Dieskau marched south, arriving at the head of the lake on September 8, 1755. The three conflicts that took place that day are known collectively as "The Battle of Lake George." In the first of these battles, Colonel Ephraim Williams, one of Johnson's three regimental commanders, was killed. Colonel Williams' will provided for the founding of Williams College.

Having served in Massachusetts during King George's War as a captain, Colonel Williams had moved his men from Fort Edward (then Fort Lyman) to the head of Lake George where they were waiting for boats to be built to take them north across the lake. Early on the morning of September 8th, Baron Dieskau, leading a French war party of about 2,000 men, effectively ambushed Johnson's 1,000 British and colonial

"I am building a fort at this lake where no house ever before was built, nor a rod of land cleared, which the French call Lake St. Sacrement, but I have given it the name of Lake George, not only in honor of His Majesty, but to ascertain his undoubted dominion here."

Sir William Johnson
September 3, 1755

troops and 200 Mohawks, led by Colonel Williams, about three miles from Lake George. Along with Colonel Williams, a well-liked Mohawk chief, King Hendrick, was also killed.

Around 11:00 a.m. Dieskau then attacked the rest of the English troops, that were by then dug in at their camp ("the Massachusetts men on the right, and the Connecticut men on the left"). This attack was disastrous to the French. Dieskau himself was seriously wounded and captured. Only the personal guard of Johnson and 50 trusted English soldiers prevented the Indians from killing Dieskau in revenge for the morning attack during which several well-liked chiefs had been killed.

At about 5:00 p.m., the French and their Indian allies were resting next to a pond after having plundered and scalped the dead at the scene of the morning's ambush. An English scouting party surprised them. Although heavily outnumbered, the English inflicted heavy casualties on the French. The bodies of the dead French and Indians were thrown into the pond that is still called "Bloody Pond."

The fighting that took place on September 8th involved at least eleven Wilbraham men. Lieutenant Nathaniel Burt was killed. While Lt. Burt is generally thought to be a Wilbraham soldier, he is also claimed by Longmeadow and there may, in fact, be a memorial gravestone to him in the Longmeadow Burying Yard. Lt. Burt has also been listed as a Springfield resident.

Although the Crown Point expedition was a failure, mostly due to Johnson's hesitation following the ambush by Dieskau, Johnson achieved considerable notoriety. This fame allowed him to establish Fort William Henry at Lake George and to rename the lake itself from the French Lac St. Sacrement. He also renamed Fort Lyman to Fort Edward.

Raids continued throughout 1756-1757 and the French garrison at Fort Carillon, later renamed Fort Ticonderoga, was often under attack. By then, General Johnson was building Fort William Henry at the head of the lake. Named for the Duke of Cumberland, King George III's brother, the fort successfully withstood a five-day siege in March of 1757. The following August saw the fort surrendered to General Montcalm by Lieutenant Colonel George Munro after a lengthy siege. Although given assurance of safe passage by Montcalm, the Indians attacked the English party, killing and scalping some and taking others into captivity. During what is known as the "Massacre at Fort William Henry." Following the massacre, General Montcalm had the fort destroyed and a great funeral pyre built from the logs. He then set off to the north again.

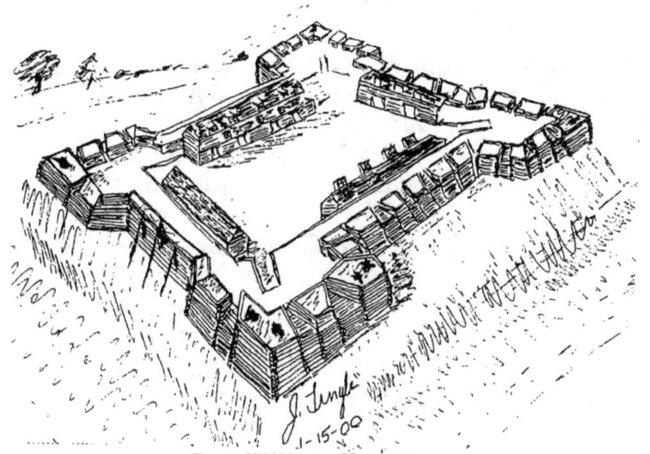

Fort William Henry

It was during the siege of Fort William Henry that the friendly Indians, Uncas and Hawkeye, saved Colonel Munro's two daughters by hiding them in a cave near Glens Falls. The hiding place today is known as Cooper's Cave. This incident served as background material for James Fenimore Cooper's The Last of the Mohicans.

During the time of the French and Indian War, many of the soldiers were American Provincials, that is, local militiamen. The British regulars were too few in numbers to wage major battles but served as the leadership for the Provincial units. The majority of the support units, such as artillery and engineers, were regular British units. As might be expected, the colonial soldiers were also given the majority of the heavy labor so as to keep the regulars well rested. For very little food, water, or pay, the Provincials cut the roads, felled the lumber, built the forts, and, of course, fought and died, while their families stayed at home alone, often with no defense against marauding bands of Indians.

The Second Expedition to Crown Point 1759

The second expedition to take Ticonderoga and Crown Point began seriously in 1759. This would coincide with the capture of Quebec and the end of the war.

The army moved from Fort Edward to Lake George by the end of June 1759. By then there were about eleven thousand men in the army, about half were British regulars and half were Provincials. Their days at Lake George were spent drilling, firing by platoons and practicing maneuvers, scouting the area, and foraging for wood and hay. The surgeon also required the men to go down to the lake whenever the weather permitted to wash (their hands and faces at least).

According to Francis Parkman's "Montcalm and Wolfe," courts-martial were common and floggings handed out regularly. Occasionally a man was shot for his crimes.

An ongoing task was the cutting of the tops of spruce trees to make spruce beer. It was thought that this drink protected one against scurvy and a generous supply of West Indian molasses was kept on hand to ensure a good supply of beer. Samuel Warner's Journal is quoted by Parkman as saying the men could have as much as they wanted for a halfpenny a quart.

While the beer may or may not have done much for scurvy, I would suspect it did wonders to alleviate the tedium of camp life – taken for medicinal purposes only, of course.

The army left their encampment and marched to Ticonderoga on July 21st. On July 23rd, they discovered that all but 400 of the French had abandoned the fort. Three days later, on July 26th, the remaining French escaped and blew up part of the fort's magazine.

On August 1st the army was told that Crown Point had also been abandoned. With no forces facing him, Johnson was able to send Brigadiers Prideaux and Thomas Gage to recapture Niagara. Johnson then spent the rest of the year preparing boats for use on Lake Champlain and the St. Lawrence River for the next year's campaign.

Meanwhile, General Wolfe was on his way to Quebec. The momentous battle for Quebec came in the autumn of 1759 when Wolfe and his troops climbed the cliffs and met the French army on the Plains of Abraham. Both Wolfe and Montcalm were killed in this English victory.

The fall of Quebec is descibed as a major turning point in Amercan history. When Wolfe's army assaulted Quebec, the whole West from Quebec to New Orleans belonged to France. By the end of the following day, France had lost her hold on these lands forever. The treaty of peace in 1763 formalized the ownership of a huge portion of America by England. Even Spain, who had owned Florida for 250 years, was affected because of her support for France and was forced to turn over Florida to the English.

By the end of 1763, the flag of England flew over the entire eastern section of North America.

Samuel "Clark" Warner's Journal (1759)

Samuel Warner Sr. spent his early years on his father's farm on what is now Allen Street in Springfield. In 1733, the family moved to Wilbraham to the northwest corner of Main and Springfield Streets. After the move to Wilbraham, Samuel began keeping track of the births and deaths in the Outward Commons. For 49 years and five months, he maintained the "official" records of these events in the new town. Because of this, he is often referred to as Clark ("Clerk") Warner.

At some point, Samuel built his own home on Stony Hill Road where the present Wilbraham Country Club is located. He died while visiting his daughter in Hancock, Massachusetts, near Lebanon Springs, NY, and the site of warm springs. As his tombstone says, he died at Lebanon and it has been said that he died suddenly while at the springs.

Apart from his self-imposed duties as the town clerk, Samuel is most famous for the journal he kept while he was in the army during the French and Indian War. Having enlisted in Colonel John Worthington's regiment on June 14, 1757, he later, at the age of 51, reenlisted in Captain John Bancroft's company of Colonel Timothy Ruggles' regiment. Colonel Ruggles' regiment was a labor regiment and mostly built barracks, cleared roads, etc. Most of Samuel's journal entries refer to his work as a mason. Part of the journal Samuel kept of his time in the regiment is included in the Stebbins History. It covers his trip from Albany to Fort Edward and the time span of early June 1755 to his return to Wilbraham on November 28, 1759. This portion of the journal is also included in this document as appendix A.

As mentioned earlier, the journal is quoted in the classic reference, Montcalm and Wolfe: The French and Indian War by Francis Parkman, originally published in 1884.

Samuel's son Phanuel served in the Revolutionary War at the Lexington Alarm and later at Quebec. He died at Crown Point while in the service, some 17 years after his father and older brother served there. Another of Samuel's sons, Nathaniel Edward, also served in the Revolutionary War at the Bennington Alarm in 1777. Samuel's son Azriel was commissioned a lieutenant in the militia in 1799 and became a captain in 1803. He served in the militia until 1805.

Lastly, Samuel Jr., born on January 1, 1734 enlisted with his father for the French and Indian War and served with him at Ticonderoga and Crown Point. He also responded to the Lexington Alarm in 1775 and then again served 99 days at Ticonderoga during the Revolution between December 1776 and April 1777. Samuel Jr's son Seth also served in the Revolution.

The "Louisburg Expedition"

The only "firm" listing I could find that correlates to those Wilbraham men previously identified by our local histories is a report in the Journal of the New England Historical Society on the Louisburg Expedition of 1745 (NEHS, July 1871).

Unfortunately, this report seems to be at odds with previous documents in that it states that these men served in the Ninth Regiment under Colonel, possibly General, Dwight who raised a regiment of Connecticut Valley soldiers following his return from Louisburg. This regiment was raised for a planned expedition against Canada. Their destination was changed, however, and instead they erected Fort Massachusetts. Our previous histories state that George Mygate and Rueben Hitchcock both died in the expedition to Louisburg. As both of their names appear in the Ninth Regiment, it would seem they may have died at Fort Massachusetts, rather than at Louisburg.

It would appear that at least the following men from Wilbraham served in Dwight's Ninth Regiment:

Jonathan Ball	5th & 10th Company - died in Wilbraham in 1760
Capt. Isaac Colton	6th Company
Rueben Hitchcock	5th & 10th Company - died in the army
Benjamin Knowlton	5th, 6th, 10th Company
George Mygate	5th & 10th Company - died in the army
James Shaw	1st & 10th Company
James Warriner	5th Company

An Ensign Thomas Jones is also listed. He may have been the father of the Thomas Jones who is credited with building a house on Main Street in 1755. In fact, the Lt. Thomas Jones who is given credit for building the house was born in 1739 and would only have been 16 years old when the house was built. It seems likely that the builder was actually this Ensign Thomas Jones or that the house was not built in 1755.

There may have been others from Wilbraham in this list but as many of the names of the time were common to our entire county (Warriner, Hitchcock, etc.) it is not possible to determine which town they were from.

Fort Ticonderoga - King George's War

Wilbraham soldiers who served on active duty during and shortly after King George's War:

- Aaron Bliss - Part of military expedition to Hatfield in August 1748 for 58 days under Capt. Isaac Colton.
- Isaac Colton - Captain in August 1748 on 58 day expedition to Hatfield.
- Samuel Day - Served at Ft. Massachusetts May 27 & 28 1747 under Col. John Stoddard. Green Mountain Patrols in 1749. Became Lieutenant in 1749 and Captain in August 1754 at age 56.
- Paul Langdon - Served at Ft. Massachusetts 5/19-6/10/1747 and at Fort Shirley 12/10/1747-5/18/1748 and again 6/11-10/31/1748.
- Thomas Merrick - Was Ensign in March 1749 on Green Mountain Patrols.
- James Shaw - Green Mountain Patrols in 1749.

Miscellaneous Service in the French & Indian War

- John Hitchcock, 3rd - Served on Western Frontier of Massachusetts (9/2-9/12/1754) under Captain Isaac Colton.
- John Jones - Listed in Copeland's History of Hampden County as having been at Quebec in 1757. A memorial stone in Adams Cemetery in Wilbraham says he died at Quebec in 1757 at age 21.
- Captain Isaac Colton - Served on Western Frontier of Massachusetts (9/2-9/12/1754) and, at age 57, commanded a company at Louisburg in 1757.
- Isaac Colton, 3rd - Wrote his will on June 14, 1759 in case he didn't return. He died at Crown Point.
- Timothy Wright - Served at Fort #4 under Captain William Williams (9/11/1754 - 2/26/1755).
- Nathaniel Sikes - Buried in Adams Cemetery, he died at Fort Edward in 1760, most likely on garrison duty. No other records have been found of his service.
- Ebeneezer Cadwell - His powder horn, signed with his name, the date 1758, and "Fort Edward" is in the possesion of his Great (4th) Grand Daughter in New Hampshire. Ebeneezer also marched at the Lexington Alarm in 1775.

French & Indian War

First Crown Point Expedition in 1755

Wilbraham men from "A List of 151 men Voluntarily Inlisted into his Majesty's Service for reinforcing the Army for Crown Point out of y[e] Southern Regiment in the County of Hampshire,"

- John Langdon
- Timothy Wright
- Philip Lyon, Private
- William King, Jr.

These men were called to duty for three months.

Lake George Campaign Sometime Before October 1, 1755

- Samuel Day, Captain.
- Henry Chapin, Lieutenant
- John Hitchcock, Lieutenant
- William King, Private
- John Langdon, Private
- Timothy Wright, Private

Baron Dieskau Battle - September 8, 1755

These men were in the battle near the southern extremity of Lake George (near Fort William Henry with Baron Dieskau. They served in Captain Luke Hitchcock's (from Springfield) company from April 1755 to January 1756. Their enlistment dates are also shown below:

- Lt. Nathaniel Burt - Killed in this battle
- Daniel Cadwell – Sergeant – 4/15 to 12/11
- Paul Langdon - Sergeant – 4/19 to 12/9
- Aaron Parsons, Sergeant – 4/11 to 10/1
- Isaac Colton, Corporal – 4/11 to 11/27
- Aaron Bliss, Corporal – 5/5 to 10/1
- Aaron Alvord - Private – 4/11 to 9/29
- Stephen Bliss – Private – 5/5 to 12/9
- Benjamin Warriner, Private – 4/11 – 10/1
- Jesse Warner, Private – 4/15 to 12/9
- Samuel "Clark" Warner, Private – 4/11 to 10/1
- Aaron Warriner, Private – 4/11 to 10/1
- Benjamin Wright, Private – 4/19 to 9/22

French & Indian War

Second Expedition to Crown Point - 1759

Capt. John Bancroft's company, Col. Timothy Ruggles' Regiment.

- Benoni Atchinson, Private
- Moses Bartlett, Private
- Thomas Dunham, Private
- Paul Hitchcock, Private
- Moses Warriner, Private
- Samuel Warner, Sr., Private
- Samuel Warner, Jr., Private - Stebbins says Samuel Jr. died in 1751 but this is not true. Samuel Jr. was also at Lexington.

From 1863 Stebbins History.

Samuel Warner's Journal

Based on the portions of Samuel Warner's journal reprinted in Stebbins' history book, one can ascertain that the following were also in camp with Samuel Warner, Sr. at various times:

- Samuel, Jr. - his son
- Benoni Atchinson , June 7
- Isaac Whittemore, June 7
- William Hancock, July 18
- Abner Parsons, July 18
- "*Hitchcock was killed*"*, October 11
- William Harris, Died October 19
- Aaron Prest, Died October 29

* This reference to Hitchcock might well refer to a Hitchcock not from Wilbraham. In any event, I haven't been able to develop any other references for a Hitchcock with him during this timeframe.

III. The Revolution

Preface

Wilbraham's military involvement in the American Revolution began with the Lexington Alarm. An obvious shift in the way the army was to be populated took place following the first two years of the conflict. Initially, the period was marked by call-ups of the local enrolled militia as units, such as was done for Lexington and Bennington. Starting in 1778, however, men who served in our area were drafted or enlisted as individuals. The "volunteer" militia would appear to have been a viable concept for protecting settlements against Indian attacks while not very effective in a prolonged active campaign against an enemy such as Great Britain.

The first two years, in fact, marked the end of the effective use of our local militia units as actual companies. While they would continue to exist until the Commonwealth assumed control of all military affairs in 1840, September 1777 appears to be the last time a Wilbraham company, as a military unit, was activated for an actual military campaign. This is probably due to the fact that no direct threat to the New England states was perceived following Burgoyne's surrender at Saratoga in October 1777.

The Timeline

Overview

Massachusetts has been called the hotbed of the Revolution. Given our current environment, it is difficult to imagine what everyday life in Wilbraham as a farming community was like and the stress that must have been felt while a war was fought all around it. The residents had to accommodate the daily rigors of farming while also maintaining their readiness to take off on very short notice to fight.

Given their everyday responsibilities to their families, I have found it noteworthy that so many of our men joined the army, if only for short time. While it might be interesting to try to ascribe motives to some of the men, especially those who seemed to make a career out of the war, it is probably more likely that no motive can be given other than that it was just a different time and they were different people than we are today.

In 1765, the British Parliament passed the Stamp Act. That act was intended to help pay for the recent French and Indian War and to cover the cost of the ten thousand troops the king wanted to send to protect the colonies from further Indian or French attacks. The law required the colonies to use stamps on all law and business papers, pamphlets, and newspapers. The Act was denounced throughout America and when the stamps finally arrived the colonists destroyed them.

When news of this disobedience arrived in England, the Stamp Act was quickly repealed in 1766. Soon after this, Massachusetts set up its own independent government and appointed John Hancock to be its head. Samuel Adams also organized "Committees of Correspondence" through the towns could consult on public matters by letters. Starting with Virginia in 1773, the other colonies soon established their own committees. This eventually led to the calling of a Continental Congress.

For the rest of this section, I will be covering the major events in Massachusetts as relate to the formation of the army and, wherever possible, tying in local and national events to those dates. This is to establish a timeline for Wilbraham's military involvement in the conflict and to put our involvement into the context of the overall struggle.

June/July 1774 - At Town Meetings held on June 23rd and July 29th, with Major John Bliss as moderator, the people voted £25 to provide a town stock of ammunition and powder. The July meeting produced an agreement to stop all trade with Great Britain and to buy no British goods. The agreement, the Non-Consumption Pledge, also stipulated that no one was to buy products from anyone in town who did not sign the pledge. Paul Langdon was the first to sign, followed by 124 of his fellow townsmen.

Missing from the signers is Phineas Newton who appeared as a Lieutenant in Town Meeting minutes in 1773 and who held minor town offices until the spring of 1774. His name no longer appears in town records after this although he again appears as a lieutenant on Captain Carpenter's company of Guards in 1778.

Also at the June Town Meeting, the members agreed to "take into consideration...the Present Distressed condition of this Insulted Province."

October 1774 - The Massachusetts' Provincial Congress organized at Concord. A resolution was passed on October 26th that made provision in the towns for a Committee of Safety with the authority to "alarm, muster, and cause to be assembled" a militia force "completely armed" to defend the province. This resolution also directed the militia units be formed into companies of at least fifty privates to be held "in Readiness on the shortest notice." This directive, then, established the "Minute Men." This set the stage for the towns to have one quarter of the enrolled militia companies ready to respond to an alarm at a minute's notice. Already organized and ready, the alarm lists for the Lexington Alarm are the most complete and accurate of all preserved in the Commonwealth. Also in October, on the 27th, two General officers were selected to lead the troops of the Commonwealth. They were Seth Pomeroy of Northhampton for the southern towns and Artemus Ward of Shrewsbury. John Bliss of Wilbraham was chosen as one of General Seth Pomeroy's chief aides.

Year-end 1774 - On December 10th, additional instruction was given to each town to arm each Minute Man with an "effective Fire arm, Bayonet, Pouch, Knapsack, Thirty rounds of Cartidges and Ball." They were to drill at least three times a week. It was suggested the towns pay the soldiers a "reasonable consideration." At about this time, the Hampshire militia was reorganized into four regiments, centered around Springfield, Northampton, Amherst, and Deerfield. (All of Western Massachusetts was part of Hampshire County at the time. Hampden County was not made a separate county until 1812.)

January 1775 - The Town Meeting chose Major John Bliss as a delegate to the second "provential Congress."

March 1775 - Capt. Paul Langdon prepared an inventory of all military stores.

April 19, 1775 – The British General Sir Thomas Gage, having learned that the colonists were storing arms for the militia at Concord, sent forward troops to destroy the stores. The troops were to go by way of Lexington where it was thought that Samuel Adams and John Hancock were visiting a friend. Leaving Boston just before midnight on April 18th, a signal in the Old North Church alerted Paul Revere who then set out to give the alarm. Just before daybreak on April 19th, the regulars marched into Lexington. At that point the events leading up to the "shot heard round the world" and the subsequent disastrous retreat of the regulars back to Boston began.

April 20, 1775 - At around 3:30 AM, Israel Bissell of East Windsor, CT, passed through Wilbraham to give the alarm for Gage's move on Lexington. While it is unsure how the alarm spread quickly through town, within a couple of hours after sunrise, the militia had gathered on the training field near today's Mile Tree School. This contingent moved out at around noon for Lexington with Captain James Warriner in command. Captain Warriner reported to his battalion commander, Major Andrew Colton, at Waltham, on April 24th. The company was dismissed on April 25th, returned home, and was disbanded on April 29th. The company saw no action.

April 21, 1775 – The Committee of Safety for the Commonwealth called for an army of 8,000. Locally, while part of the company was en route to Lexington under Capt. Warriner, the remainder of the company was called out on the morning of the April 20th. From the assembled men, about seventy were selected and organized by Captain Paul Langdon. They then marched to Palmer where the 1st Hampshire Regiment was assembling. The regiment then marched to Cambridge on the 21st, arriving on April 25th. On April 29th, forty-five of these men went into the Massachusetts army. Note that while both of these numbers are quite a bit higher than previous historical reports, they are also much more accurate. Capt. Langdon accepted a commission as a Lieutenant upon his enlistment and was promoted to Captain by July. James Shaw also became a lieutenant in an artillery company guarding Cambridge. Daniel Cadwell joined with Capt. Langdon and became a second lieutenant under him. The men that enlisted in the army served in the Roxbury lines until their enlistment expired and the unit was disbanded in December. At least seven (and most likely more) were sent as a detachment to Quebec on Benedict Arnold's famous march.

Those men that chose not to go into the army in April were released to their homes and returned to their enrolled militia status. Major John Bliss, Ensign Oliver Bliss and twenty-five others did not join up and returned to Wilbraham on or around May 5th.

April 23, 1775 – Apparently having reconsidered the call for 8,000 two days earlier, the Committee of Safety for the Commonwealth called for an army of 30,000 men to be raised for the colony and another 13,600 for the province.

April 26, 1775 – The Committee of Safety asked those who had not yet done so to enlist into the army. Many Wilbraham men did enlist probably based on this call. See April 21st.

April 29, 1775 – One half of each town's militia was ordered to be sent immediately to Cambridge and Roxbury with the remainder to hold themselves in readiness. Wilbraham's soldiers were assigned to the Roxbury lines.

May 10, 1775 - With the Massachusetts Army surrounding the British in and around Boston, a plan for the capture of the fortresses of Ticonderoga, Crown Point and Skeenesborough (now Whitehall) was conceived. These forts created a major route of communication between the colonies and Canada and they were extremely important targets. The fortresses were all surprised and captured, without bloodshed, by Colonels Ethan Allen and Seth Warner with the help of two hundred and thirty Green Mountain Boys and officers Dean, Wooster, Parsons and Benedict Arnold, and forty other men from Connecticut. On the evening of the 10th of May, as the invaders approached Ticonderoga, a sentinel snapped his gun at Colonel Allen and retreated. When entry into the fortress was achieved, the aged commander was found napping. Colonel Allen demanded that he immediately surrender the fort. He responded, "By what authority, sir?" Colonel Allen's reply was, "In the name of the Great Jehovah and the Continental Congress." Obviously, this was a combination of powers to be reckoned with as the fort was then surrendered.

May/June 1775 – The Minute Companies were organized provisionally for service on April 20th. They were reorganized between May 27 – June 16 as four battalions for eight months service in the Massachusetts Line. The Wilbraham men were placed in Colonel Timothy Danielson's Regiment. Danielson's Regiment consisted of eleven companies from Hampshire and Worcester counties, from Massachusetts; and New London and Hartford counties, from Connecticut. The regiment was adopted on June 14 into the Continental Army and assigned on July 22 to Thomas' Brigade, an element of the main army. It was redesignated as the 3rd Continental Regiment on January 1, 1776.

June 14, 1775 – Congress authorized the formation of the Continental Army.

July 5, 1775 – Each soldier was offered a coat as a gift or bounty for enlisting. Later, either the coat or money in lieu of the coat could be chosen by the soldier. This bounty coat is the subject of many letters at the end of the year from the various company commanders to the "cloathing" officers at Watertown. These letters ordered the coats that were to be furnished to their men.

August 14, 1775 – The merger of the Massachusetts Army into the Continental Army is formally recognized.

September 1775 - Some of the troops at Roxbury were detached in September to serve with Colonel Benedict Arnold at Quebec. Four of these men died while "on command" up north. Given the horrible conditions of Arnold's march up the Kennebec River to attack Quebec, we are lucky only four Wilbraham men perished. The march took from September 11th to November 8th. While he would have preferred not to, Arnold made the attack on December 31st since his troops' enlistments were to expire on January 1st. The attack failed and the British retained control of Quebec.

Year-end 1775 - The enrolled militia totaled about 200 at the end of 1775. About a quarter of these men had served at some point during the year. A few had re-enlisted in General Benedict Arnold's army, but most had returned home by year-end. The war in 1775 was mostly fought in the north. While the British were forced to withdraw from Boston, the American attack in Canada failed.

January 1776 - Knox's Train of Artillery
The Revolutionary Army, while energetic and well supplied with men, was lacking in artillery. The British stronghold at Ticonderoga with its supply of cannon was, therefore, an attractive target for the young army. The idea to capture Ticonderoga and move its cannon is thought to have been conceived by Colonel Henry Knox, Washington's 25-year-old chief of artillery. Ethan Allen and his Vermont Green Mountain Boys captured the Fort on May 10, 1775. After waiting until December for Lake George to freeze and an adequate blanket of snow to fall, Knox moved the cannon on "42 exceeding strong sleds" across Lake George, down along the Hudson, and then more or less along Massachusetts routes 71, 23, and 20 to Cambridge.

This was an incredible journey given the lack of roads and the freezing weather of a New England winter. Nonetheless his train of artillery passed through Wilbraham on January 15 or 16, 1776. According to the 1976 Bicentennial Revolutionary Pamphlet, the procession went up Maple Street and Mountain Road and then downhill over a stone bridge spanning Spear Brook, and then onto Boston Road near the foot of Butler Hill. The only section of the bridge still visible is a small section over which the driveway to Coed Billiards travels. Colonel Knox reported to General Washington in Boston on January 24, 1776. Soon after the cannon were positioned in Boston in March, the British evacuated the town. Colonel Knox went on to become a major general and the first Secretary of War.

January 1, 1776 – Colonel Danielson's Regiment was consolidated, less Thompson's and Egery's companies with Learned's Regiment and designated the 3rd Continental Regiment.

January 19, 1776 – A new regiment, comprised of men from Berkshire and Hampshire counties, was formed. They were to reinforce the army in Canada and serve until January 1st, 1777. Also in January, new officers for Wilbraham's enrolled militia were chosen. At this time Captain Daniel Cadwell, Jr., 1st Lieutenant William King, and 2nd Lieutenant Phineas Stebbins were elected. Apparently, according to Mr. Merrick, some political feuding resulted in Cadwell's being elevated over the older, more experienced King and for Paul Langdon's being replaced entirely. Dr. Samuel F. Merrick marched with this regiment in April to assist the Northern army. Part of his journal for this period of time is included in this book as appendix C.

February 10, 1776 – A bounty of 40 shillings was offered for the regiment formed above. This is the first direct offer of money for enlistment made in the war.

March 17, 1776 – General Howe abandoned Boston.

April/June 1776 – Various regiments were created for seacoast defense, artillery batteries, cavalry, etc. This seems to have served as a rounding out or tidying up of the structure of the army following the frantic early months. Samuel F. Merrick left Wilbraham on April 22nd to serve as a Surgeon's Mate in Colonel Elisha Porter's Hampshire Regiment reinforcing the Northern Army in their retreat from Quebec.

April 15, 1776 – Danielson's Regiment was assigned to the Canadian Department.

May 1776 - The Company was split into a South Company (Hampden) and a North company (Wilbraham). Later in the year, the companies were given numerical designations with the North Company becoming the 7th Company and the South becoming the 12th. Officers were Capt. Daniel Cadwell, 1st Lt. William King, and 2nd Lt. Abel King in the North and Capt. Phineas Stebbins, 1st Lt. Noah Stebbins, and 2nd Lt. Gideon Kibbe in the South.

June 1776 - The legislature ordered 754 men to be raised for a Hampshire regiment to serve in the Northern army. Wilbraham's quota was 24 men. These men served at Ticonderoga from early July through December. Eight Wilbraham men died from disease while in this command.

July 1776 – A draft of every 25th man on the alarm list was authorized. These men were to serve until December 1, 1776 (six months). The first actual draft in the war, it was used to raise two regiments for "Northern Department" or Canada. This draft was enforced by the imposition of a £10 fine on anyone who should "neglect or refuse" to serve (or who couldn't provide someone to go in his place).

Danielson's Regiment was assigned to the Northern Department in Benedict Arnold's Brigade.

August 1776 - One in every twenty-five of the remaining enrolled militia was called for garrison duty in Dorchester. Also in August, Capt. James Shaw formed an artillery company (a company of matrosses) with Noah Stebbins as his lieutenant. An elite company, decked out in distinctive uniforms, it went into action only once during its five-year existence.

August 27, 1776 – In April and May, General Washington moved the army from Boston to New York. On August 22, General Howe landed in force on Long Island. The battle for Long Island on August 27th was a disaster for the Americans. Fortunately, Howe's failure to follow-up the attack allowed the Americans to escape throughout the night across the East River to Manhattan Island.

September 1776 – On the 12th, a draft for two months of every 5th able-bodied man under 50 years old was made, exempting those in certain occupations. Also in September, an unsuccessful attempt was made to remove Lt. William King and Mr. Enos Stebbins from the Committee of Correspondence as they were "Suspected of faithlessness in heart or weaknes in knee." Samuel F. Merrick's Journal ended on September 16th.

October 1776 – In the spring, the British had pursued the Americans down Lake Champlain with the intention of continuing down the Hudson. Brigadier General Arnold built a fleet of small boats and was able to successfully delay the British advance, stopping them at Crown Point in mid-October. With winter approaching, the British withdrew to their winter quarters in Canada.

November 1776 - Danielson's Regiment was assigned to Vose's Brigade in the Main Army.

November 14, 1776 – One quarter of all men, 16 years and older, were drafted for three months "readiness." If they were not called into actual service by March 1, 1777 they would no longer be liable for service. The various calls for one in twenty-five, one quarter, etc. must have been interesting from a mathematical standpoint. A casual reading of the various orders makes one wonder if they took into account previous drafts as the total seems at times to add up to more than one hundred percent of a town's available manpower.

December 1776 – On the fifth, sixteen companies were formed to serve for three years to replace those at Boston whose terms were expiring. The previous short-term enlistments were proving to be very burdensome on the army if, for no other reason, by the time a man got trained in the ways of the army, his enlistment was up. Also in December, Capt. Daniel Cadwell left for duty with the Northern army and Lt. William King assumed command of the Wilbraham militia. King continued in this role until the spring of 1780 with no increase in rank. Another 25 men were formed into a provisional company under Captain Daniel Cadwell, Jr., for garrison duty at Ticonderoga. They served until April 2, 1777. During a smallpox epidemic, Captain Cadwell and Sergeant Joseph Abbott died.

The first major victory for the American Army occurred on December 26th. Known as the Battle of Trenton, but more readily recognized as when Washington crossed the Delaware, this attack caught the Hessians by surprise (and quite hungover from Christmas celebrations). This effort resulted in most of New Jersey being cleared of the enemy and was a tremendous boost to American morale.

January 1777 - Danielson's Regiment was consolidated with with the 25th Continental Regiment and designated as Greaton's Regiment.

January 26, 1777 – "One seventh (here we go again) of each male member of each town" (I assume they meant each seventh male) is drafted for three years. This draft was noteworthy (apart from the wording) as it exempted no one except the Quakers. At the beginning of 1777, the authorized strength of the army was 76,000. Only 8,000 men were actually serving, however. The British strategy for this year was again to split the colonies in two by having the British forces in Canada join with those in New York at Albany. Britain would then control the Hudson River and would effectively cut New England off from the other states. Accordingly, Howe was to advance to the north in June while General John Burgoyne was to march south from Canada. Howe, unfortunately for the British, changed his mind and instead moved south towards Philadelphia.

February 1777 - Greaton's Regiment was assigned to the Northern Army again.

March 1777 - Greaton's Regiment was assigned to the Highlands Department.

April 30, 1777 – 1,500 men from Hampshire County were ordered to Fort Ticonderoga to serve for two months. These men would replace the regiment sent in December 1776 that included Captain Cadwell and his men.

May 15, 1777 – As the draft of January 26th was not working very well, an odd inducement was offered to those who had enlisted. They could serve until January 10th, 1778, for three years, or for the duration of the war. Perhaps the feeling was that the war wouldn't last three years, but I'm not entirely sure this was true. In any event, the logic behind this offer escapes me.

June 1777 - Several Wilbraham soldiers served in the regiment raised by Col. Elisha Porter, Hampshire's Sheriff, in June. This outfit served for six months. Burgoyne continued his push south, putting severe pressure on the American northern outposts. Burgoyne's force consisted of 7,200 British regulars, 250 Canadians, and 400 Indians. They were initially opposed at Ticonderoga by only 2,500 Continental soldiers and militia.

June 12, 1777 - Greaton's Regiment was assigned to the 1st Massachusetts Brigade in the Highlands.

July 1, 1777 - The 1st Brigade was reassigned to the Northern Department.

July 2, 1777 – Ticonderoga fell to General John Burgoyne. Such militia from Hampshire and Berkshire counties as could be mustered were sent to Fort Edward and Fort Ann, New York, to reinforce the beleaguered army of the North.

August 1777 – On August 9th, following the loss of Fort Ticonderoga, a call for an additional one sixth of all males was made to reinforce the army "northward." These men were to serve until November 30th unless sooner discharged. The alarm reached Wilbraham on August 14th. A unit of about 30 men was hastily assembled under the command of Captain Thomas Stebbins. Stebbins and his men were sent to support Brigadier John Stark in his fight against a German force of 800. Known as the Battle of Bennington, Stark had won his battle and virtually annihilated the German force by the time Stebbins' men arrived. The Wilbraham men made it as far as Pittsfield and were back home within a week.

September 1777 – The first battle at Bemis Heights, between Srartoga Lake and the Hudson River occurred on September 19th and was a victory for the Americans although the final outcome was still in doubt. Capt. James Shaw's volunteer artillery company of over 50 men was detached from its regiment, on September 15th for duty with Col. Porter on the Hudson River. The company mustered at Springfield on September 24th, left West Springfield on the 30th, and arrived at Stillwater, NY on October 6th. They reached their assigned positions on the east bank of the Hudson just above the present day Schuylerville on October 9th and were dismissed on the 18th, one day after Burgoyne surrendered. The unit saw no action.

Burgoyne's advance against the Americans under General Gates in mid-September resulted in the total Wilbraham alarm list's being called up. While no list of men has been found, Wilbraham's two companies mustered at Springfield under Capt. Phineas Stebbins on October 3rd. John Bliss was selected as Colonel of this regiment; with Thomas Stebbins as 2nd Major.

October 1777 - Captain Shaw's unit arrived and was directed by Col. Porter to set up just south of the mouth of the Battenkill River, near Schuylerville, NY. By October 7th, Gates had more than 10,000 men in line to oppose the British. On October 7th, the British and American armies engaged at Stillwater, just south of Bemis Heights, after which the British withdrew to near Saratoga. Burgoyne finally surrendered his men, their number now down to 5,000, on October 17th.

Dr. Samuel Merrick served as a private soldier in this unit, kept a journal that was quoted in both the Peck and Stebbins histories. This section of Dr. Merrick's journal and additional correspondence with Col. Joseph Trumbull of Connecticut is included in this book as Appendix D.

The Wilbraham unit, Dr. Merrick at least, watched General Burgoyne's surrender at Saratoga. (See Appendix D – Samuel Merrick's Journal.) The unit had fired not a single shot and was released on October 18th. The soldiers received a penny per mile for the 140 miles trip back home. Colonel Bliss also marched his regiment to Stillwater, NY, but, as with Shaw's men, the emergency was over before they arrived. Colonel Bliss's men were dismissed even before Burgoyne surrendered.

November 1777 - Under the terms of surrender at Saratoga, the British troops were to be sent to England as the "Army of Convention" and not as prisoners. Leaving Saratoga, they traveled along the route Colonel Knox had taken and passed through Wilbraham on November 1st. However, because of a shortage of food and fuel, the British General Henry Clinton notified Congress that he would no longer pay for the maintenance of the British troops. Congress declared the agreement broken and preceded to move the troops to

Charlottesville, Virginia. The British troops then became prisoners of war.

As with the capture of Quebec in the French and Indian War, the American victory at Saratoga has been deemed one of the most significant battles in our history. It resulted in completely breaking up the British plans for the war and it led directly to France, Britain's old enemy, recognizing and giving aid to the beleagured Americans.

Although General Burgoyne had since been returned to the British army at Newport, Rhode Island, and was no longer involved with his troops, some 4,145 of his men left Boston on November 9, 1778. They followed the path they had traveled earlier and were stopped in Wilbraham on November 17th so that they would not be allowed to get near the Springfield Armory. They spent the night in Wilbraham presumably near the center of town according to the Wilbraham Bicentennial pamphlet. Their route then continued south through town and into Enfield where they crossed the Connecticut River into Suffield.

March 26, 1778 – Wilbraham's Town Meeting rejected the proposed state constitution by a vote of 24 – 51. Lt. John Hitchcock and Dr. Samuel F. Merrick were chosen as delegates to the new convention to be held in 1779.

March 31, 1778 - The 1st Brigade with Greaton's Regiment was reassigned to the Highlands.

April 20, 1778 – Burgoyne's surrender at Saratoga seemed to have calmed things a bit as the next draft was for a term of only nine months, the time to begin following the men's arrival at Fishkill, New York (travel time not included for this draft). As it had become harder to raise troops by this time, penalties for non-compliance were raised to £100, to be incurred directly by the towns. This was a significant amount of money and served as a suitable inducement for the towns to work hard to fill their quotas. Because most of the conflict now centered around the southern states and the local populace felt no perceptible threat and had already suffered through three years of alarms and drafts, Colonel Bliss had an increasingly hard time filling the draft quotas.

June 12, 1778 – 1,800 men were detached to serve either at Rhode Island or northward until January 1, 1779. By mid-July, about 10,000 men were in Rhode Island keeping the British garrison at Newport penned in and "out of trouble."

December 1778 - The town of Wilbraham voted to pay any fines imposed upon the officers for their failure to raise men for the Continental Army.

February 1779 – A company of fifty men, in successive three month enlistments, was authorized to be formed to guard stores at Springfield. Similar companies were authorized for Rutland, VT, and Boston. Captain John Carpenter of Wilbraham commanded the Springfield Company.

May 1779 – A virtual stalemate existed in the North. This stayed this way until the end of the war. Strong positions were established at and around West Point and north along the Hudson River.

June 9, 1779 – 2,000 men, to be raised by "draft lot, or voluntary enlistment" were enlisted for nine months service. The Battle of Monmouth, NJ, was fought and became the last major battle in the North.

August 1, 1779 - The 1st Brigade with Greaton's Regiment was redesignated the 3rd Massachusetts Regiment.

October 9, 1779 – Another 2,000 men were called for three months service.

June 5, 1780 – A call for 3,964 men, for six months service, was made. The fine for not serving when called is now raised to £150.

June 22, 1780 – Another 4,726 men were raised to serve at Claverack on the Hudson River.

December 2, 1780 – Suffering again from the previous short-term enlistment strategy, a "patriotic appeal" was made for a voluntary enlistment of 4,240 men to serve for three years. A bounty of $50 for each man was promised to each town that filled its quota on or before June 1, 1781. Starting with this "draft," the inhabitants of towns were allowed to form themselves into classes, or groups, to procure soldiers. The class would receive the same bounty as the man enlisted. This allowed groups of people ("classes") to get together and make a profit from getting soldiers to enlist.

January 1, 1779 - The 3rd Massachusetts Regiment was assigned to the 3rd Massachusetts Brigade.

February 26, 1781 – The class system of December 1780, having proved to be very successful, was again used to raise troops for three years.

February 28, 1781 – 1,200 men were raised to serve at Rhode Island for forty days.

June 15, 1781 – 500 men were detached to serve at Rhode Island for five months.

June 30, 1781 – 2,700 men were raised to reinforce West Point and the surrounding area.

October 17, 1781 – The British General Lord Charles Cornwallis surrendered at Yorktown, Virginia after an effective siege by French and American troops. The day before they surrendered, the British encampment received an astounding 3,600 cannon shot from determined and well-supplied revolutionary forces.

March 8, 1782 – In the last draft necessary for the war, 1,500 men were to be raised for three years. This time, however, the towns were instructed to intermix the "poor with the Rich" (note the capital R) to make the classes more equal (e.g. let the poor folk make some money too).

April/June 1782 – Several resolves were issued asking the towns to comply with the March 8th call, which had proved to be quite unsuccessful. There were no more calls for troops after this although there were calls for the assembly of a few militia groups. The militia was needed to put down disturbances in Northhampton caused by the protests of what would turn into Shay's Rebellion in 1787. These units, including some Wilbraham men, were also used to retake Samuel Ely, a fiery dissenter, who had been rescued from the Springfield jail by the rioters.

June 12, 1783 - The 3rd Massachusetts Regiment was reassigned to the 1st Brigade.

Summary

The major events of the American Revolution took place over the seven years from April 19th, 1774 until Cornwallis' surrender on October 17, 1781. While Wilbraham men enlisted or were drafted in small numbers throughout the war, the large call-ups of the locally enrolled militia as a unit started with Lexington in 1775 and ended with Captain Shaw at Bennington in September 1777. The surrender of Burgoyne at Saratoga in October 1777 was also the last time New England was directly threatened by a British invasion.

Throughout the war, the Continental Army never reached its authorized strength. The ongoing call-ups of the various local militia units to supplement the army's strength made it possible for us to fight the British at all. While the militia was not as well trained as the Continentals, they were enthusiastic and quite effective when utilized properly.

As seems apparent in the early years, the original Danielson's Regiment spent most of its time bouncing between assignments in the Northern and Highlands departments. In the official U.S. Army Lineage, the 3rd Continental Regiment (Danielson's) is credited with the following engagements:

- Siege of Boston
- Defense of Canada
- Lake Champlain
- Northern New Jersey
- Saratoga

Unfortunately, with the exception of the Siege of Boston (April-December 1775) and Saratoga (the Bennington Alarm) it is impossible to tell which of our Wilbraham men served in these engagements although many obviously did as the majority of our men served in the 3rd Regiment.

On November 3, 1783 the regiment was disbanded at West Point, NY.

Captains and Other VIP's

Captain John Carpenter (1751 - 1818)

Captain John Carpenter, who lived at 585 Glendale Road in Hampden, marched at the Lexington Alarm on April 20, 1775 to Roxbury as a sergeant in Captain James Sherman's company and served seven days there. This service was credited to the Town of Brimfield. He enlisted on April 24th and on May 27th was commissioned a lieutenant in Captain Joseph Thompson's company in Colonel Timothy Danielson's Hampshire Regiment. He then served as a 1st Lieutenant in Colonel Danforth Keyes' regiment at Rhode Island from June 27, 1775 until January 4, 1778.

On May 26, 1778, he was commissioned a Captain in Colonel Ezra Wood's 3rd Worcester County regiment and on June 23rd was detached for service at Peekskill, NY, at the North River. He was discharged after this duty on February 2nd, 1779.

On March 5th, 1779, he became the commander of a company guarding stores at Springfield. Commanding mostly series of 3-months draftees, he served in this capacity through the end of March 1781. On April 1, 1781, Captain Carpenter formed a company of men previously rejected from other service. Although unable to serve in the regular lines, these men were in good enough shape to serve as garrison soldiers at forts. Captain Carpenter served as their commander for about three years and was discharged on March 31st, 1783.

Captain Carpenter is also credited with building a school at 320 Glendale Road in Hampden with Jonah Beebe in 1796. He is buried in the Glendale Cemetery in Wilbraham.

Captain James Warriner (1725 - 1795)
He previously fought in the King George's War as a replacement for the army at Louisburg in 1745. In 1754, he saw service in the French and Indian War. Captain Warriner lead the Wilbraham Minute Men at the Lexington Alarm on April 20, 1775 at the age of 50. Captain Warriner was the Town Clerk at that time. The Lexington Alarm marked his last military service. He was Town Clerk for the periods 1773 - 1778 and also 1781 - 1785. Captain Warriner died in 1795 and is buried at Adams Cemetery in Wilbraham.

Captain Daniel Cadwell (1733 - 1777)
Captain Cadwell is listed in the Church records as having been a sergeant in 1754. He also served in the French and Indian War along with his brother Ebeneezer and lived on Ridge Road in Wilbraham. He marched on April 20, 1775, with Captain Paul Langdon in Colonel Timothy Danielson's Regiment to Roxbury and enlisted into the army on April 24th. His name appears on the muster rolls of May 17th, May 22nd, and October 6th. Congress commissioned him as a second lieutenant on May 27, 1775. He became captain of the 7th Co. 1st Hampshire (Colonel Pynchon's) Regiment on May 2, 1776 (commissioned June 13th). Eunice (his wife) names him in a June 2, 1777 petition for expenses due for the removal of Captain Cadwell and some men to Skeensborough. They had caught smallpox at Ticonderoga in January 1777. He apparently died of smallpox in 1777.

Samuel F. Merrick (1751 – 1836)
Two journals and correspondence about his service with to Colonel Joseph Trumbull of Connecticut are contained in this book as appendices C, D, and E. Events in the longer journal from 1776, are amplified somewhat in his letter to Trumbull describing the retreat of the army from the north. Dr. Merrick remained active in Wilbraham affairs throughout his life. It was he who developed the first Wilbraham history, given as an address to the town in 1813. He is buried in Adams Cemetery. His great-great-grandson, Charles Merrick, wrote the 1963 town history. His great-great-great-grandson Lewellyn Merrick still lives in the family home on Main Street in Wilbraham and raises some of the finest vegetables in the area on his farm.

Captain Paul Langdon (1725 – 1804)
Captain Paul Langdon was the son of Lieutenant Paul Langdon who had served in the French and Indian War. He was appointed lieutenant in a new militia company on July 29, 1774 and became its captain in March of 1775. After the Lexington Alarm was received and Captain Warriner marched off with Wilbraham's Minutemen, the 49 year-old captain assembled a second contingent of men and on April 20, 1775 and marched them to Palmer where they assembled with the rest of the 1st Hampshire Regiment. The regiment then marched on to Cambridge and the Roxbury lines. After serving with his troops in both Roxbury and for a short time at Quebec, Captain Langdon and his unit were discharged in December 1775. He continued to serve as the Captain of the 12th Company (Hampden) through the end of 1776.

Captain Langdon died in 1804 at the age of 79 and is buried in the Old Yard in Hampden.

Sergeant John Langdon
Also the son of Lieutenant Paul Langdon, John served as a sergeant in his brother Paul's company as it answered the Lexington Alarm and while it served at Roxbury. His brother Lewis and his son John Wilson Langdon served next to him during these engagements. John is also credited by the D.A.R. with raising an independent company in Jackson's Regiment at Boston but I do not believe this is so. The "Captain" John Langdon was a relative but, based on my research into the Langdon genealogy, does not appear to be the John Langdon from Wilbraham.

The following letter from John Langdon was sent while John served in the Roxbury lines under his brother, Captain Paul Langdon.

ROXBURY CAMP July ye 24th 1775
Dear wife these Comes with my tender affection to you hoping they will find you all well. Through the great goodness of almighty God I am in a good Steat of helth for which I desier to be thankfull their was a man shot through the breast with a musket ball and Expired that night it was Joseph wood that lived with mr. Brown last summer he was shot last Thursday

night. *[Note: this was Joseph Wood from Mendon (possibly Upton) who marched on the Lexington Alarm and enlisted into the army on May 5th.]* last Thursday a Part of our men with the whale Boats went to the light house and burnt it tuck five prisenors one boat and burnt another tuck two Swevels guns they broke of the lamps two barrels of powder two of oyl without the loss of a man there is a great deal of news in the Camp but I cant write more. I see Majr Bliss he told me you ware well.

I should be glad to have a pair of white lenen breaches my old Sockens are worn out almost I would have hier Som help to do your haying and the harvest all do as well as you can and the Lord bless you all.

My love to my dear Children John & James be good boys and be kind to your mother no more but I remain your most affectionate Husband

JOHN
LANGDON

my duty to my hon[d] mother & all friends in heast.

Sergeant John Langdon died October 10th, 1832 and is buried in the Old Yard in Hampden.

Major Thomas Stebbins
Thomas Stebbins was the captain of a company of 68 men raised in Wilbraham, Springfield, and West Springfield for Roxbury and is listed in a company roll dated January 18, 1776 for Colonel Learned's Continental Regiment. Stebbins was commissioned on February 1, 1776. He led a group of about 30 men northward to respond to the Bennington Alarm. He was promoted by the House of Representatives to Second Major on October 3, 1777 for Colonel Bliss's Regiment.

Captain James Shaw (1739 - 1831)
Captain Shaw enlisted on May 5th, 1775. The son of Second Lieutenant James Shaw, a veteran of Cape Breton in King George's War, James was the captain of an artillery company under Colonel Charles Pynchon in August 1776. He served as a private under Captain Daniel Cadwell at Ticonderoga in December 1776. He also formed a volunteer artillery company in mid-1777. This company was sent to Saratoga on September

15, 1777. Captain Shaw died on April 8, 1831 and is buried at Adams Cemetery in Wilbraham.

Lieutenant Colonel Abel King (1743 - 1812)
Abel King lived on Glendale Road in Hampden. He marched on the Lexington Alarm in Captain Warriner's Company on April 20, 1775. He was commissioned a second lieutenant in Captain Cadwell's 7th Company on June 13, 1776 and became its captain on July 16, 1779. He served as captain of the 7th Company through at least April 16, 1780. He was also the captain of a company in Colonel Sears' Regiment at Saratoga from July 23, 1781 though November 20, 1781. Promoted to Lieutenant Colonel in 1782, he served in that capacity until 1787.

Sheriff Asaph King (1747 – 1834)
In 1778, Asaph King was listed as a forager under Captain Abel King. Captain King appointed him Assistant Forage Master with the rank of Lieutenant. He also is mentioned in a letter from 1782 for payment of wages assigned him for Joseph Cutt of Wilbraham and served in the Rhode Island campaign. After the war he became the sheriff for Wilbraham and is credited with a ride through "waist deep" snow to warn General Shepard of the imminent arrival of Daniel Shay's rebellious troops in 1787. He was granted a pension for his war service at age 86. Born in Enfield, CT, Sheriff King died on October 19, 1834 at age 88 and is buried in Adams Cemetery in Wilbraham.

Colonel John Bliss (1727 - 1809)
John Bliss, II, served as a selectman, state representative, senator, and judge. He was a delegate to three provincial congresses and a Captain in the new militia company formed on July 29, 1774. He was then promoted to Major in August. He marched with Capt. Paul Langdon to Roxbury and served four days. He was commissioned a lieutenant colonel on February 8, 1776 to replace Colonel Pynchon, who had resigned. He was regimental commander of the 1st Regiment, Brigadier General Timothy Danielson's Brigade on July 5, 1777. He served as the regiment's colonel from October 3, 1777 until 1781. According to the D.A.R., he resigned his commission due to failing health and was replaced by Gideon Burt of Longmeadow. Colonel Bliss moved from Longmeadow in 1750

to 128 Somers Rd, Hampden. In 1763, he owned the property at 142 South Rd.

Captain Gideon Kibbe
Captain Kibbe served in Captain Phineas Stebbins' company and as a lieutenant in Captain Samuel Burt's company, Colonel Elisha Porter's Regiment. Prior to May 1776, he was a subaltern. In May 1776, he was commissioned a Second Lieutenant and was made a captain in June 1776. From 1776 and after, at least through 1781, he served as a captain.

Confusions
The names contained in previous Wilbraham histories served as a starting point for research into this period. In a few cases, it was extremely difficult or impossible to find any records for soldiers named in the previous works. Even taking into account every conceivable spelling of the names, there were some that just left me confused. Examples of these are as follows.

Joshua Leech - According to our previous histories, Joshua died in 1776 in the army. The closest proof I can come up with is a soldier named John Leech who was drafted to serve on board the galley "Trumbell" in the Lake Champlain expedition in September 1776. He was killed in October 1776. The reference I found is a letter from his wife Susanna requesting aid for her and her two small children as compensation for his death. Owing to the year matching correctly, the paucity of records for 1776, and the lack of accuracy in regard to names throughout this era, I am quite comfortable with "John" being our "Joshua," but I cannot be completely sure.

Malam Dunham – Malam is listed in a Hampden history as one of five brothers who fought in the Revolution. I can find no reference to a Malam Dunham, under any spelling, in the state records.

Isaac Skinner – Previous histories say he was "killed by the Indians" during the Revolution in 1780. I was unable to find any reference to this or even his death in the state records.

Joseph Butler, George Merrick, & Josiah Wright – These three men supposedly "died in the army" in 1776. There is no corroboration for this in the "Mass. Soldiers and Sailors," but 1776 was the most incomplete year for records.

Just "Deserts"

Desertion was a problem throughout the Revolution so, while we are well represented in that group, we should not agonize too much over the numbers. The following men are listed as having been deserters:

David Allen	Phineas Mason
Bacchus Boston	William Osbon
Peleg Burdick	Henry Smith
Benjamin Glayser	James Williams
William Lamson	

Favorites

Two of the men I discovered became my favorites, Asa because of his unique enlistment and Bacchus as he is now Wilbraham's third black Revolutionary soldier.

Asa Woodworth

Asa is the only man from town I could identify as having enlisted "for the duration" of the war. He was born in Coventry, CT, and enlisted in May 1777 for Wilbraham. At age 19, he was 5'8" tall, had a light complexion and light hair. He served at Cherry Valley, Fort Alden, West Point, and the York Huts. In January 1782 after five years(!), he was given a forty day furlough. He returned from the furlough 19 days late, was court-martialed, and sentenced to 30 lashes. Fortunately, the poor soul was pardoned. He was discharged at the end of the war on June 9, 1783.

Bacchus Boston

I discovered Bacchus Boston's name in the *Massachusetts Soldiers and Sailors.* While previous Wilbraham histories acknowledge only two black revolutionary soldiers from Wilbraham (Joseph Cutt and Caeser Mirick (Merrick)), Bacchus Boston was, in fact, a third black Wilbraham soldier. Although he enlisted for Springfield on March 12, 1781, his residence is listed as Wilbraham. Enlisting for three years at age 30 and being 5'6" tall, Bacchus served in Captain Watson's Company of the 3rd Continental Regiment initially and then in Captain James Tisdale's Company, Colonel Michael Jackson's Regiment, during 1783. He deserted at Philadelphia on August 17, 1783.

Deaths

Some of the Wilbraham men died, either of disease or in battle, while in the service. The following list is the best compilation I could make based on a combination of previous town histories and the "Mass. Soldiers and Sailors" volumes:

1775	Benjamin Chub	Solomon King
1776	Joseph Butler*	Joshua Leech
	Nathaniel Miles	Phanuel Warner
	George Merrick	Aaron Bliss
	Joseph Morris	Benjamin Russell
	Josiah Wright*	
1777	Daniel Warriner	Daniel Cadwell
	Joseph Abbott	Jeremiah Bradley
1778	Samuel Lyon	
1779	Elijah Hancock	
1780	John W. Chaffee	Luther Ainsworth
	Moses Simons	Isaac Skinner*
	Daniel Woodworth	

* - Unable to confirm

The Wilbraham Vital Statistics compiled by Chauncey Peck in 1906 also shows a "Washbon – died in the army at Yorkk 1775." I could find no record of this under any spelling of this or related names.

The Lexington Alarm - April 1775

- Captain James Warriner and his Wilbraham Company "marched in defense of Ammerican (sic) Liberty on y[e] Alarm last April (1775) occasioned by the Lexington Fight with y[e] number of officers & soldiers, time of service distance from home what due to each according to his character agreeable to a late Resolve of the great and Gen[ll] court of this Colony." State Rolls 12/5/1775
- A roll submitted by Captain Warriner listed those who "Went upon the Alarm last April occasioned by Lexington fight who did not Imbody under the command of any officer, an account of y[e] time of their service distance from & to home and what due."
- Time of Service was generally ten days.
- Mileage was 180 miles except for Chaffee (60) and Jonathan Cooley (160). Money due ranged from 2 pounds, 17 Shillings, 9 Pence (£ 2.17.9) for Captain Warriner to 1 Pound, 9 Shillings, 2 Pence for the private soldiers.
- Note that John Hitchcock was 53 years old and Ezekiel Russell was either 53 or 54! Captain Warriner was 50.
- The names were attested to by Captain Warriner who wrote: "Dec[r] 5th 1775 The Persons above named living in the Town of Wilbraham who marched with their arms & ammunition occas[d] by Lexington fight some before & some came after me who pray they may have pay agreeable to a late resolve of the Gen[ll] Court of this Colony agreeable to the services that are fixd to their names which is the time and service affixt to each man in this Roll according to y[e] best of my Knowledge
  Attest JAMES WARRINER, Cap[tn]"

Aaron Alvord, Sgt
Charles Brewer
Gideon Burt
Ebeneezer Cadwell
Jesse Carpenter
Asa Chaffee
Comfort Chaffee, Sr.
Darius Chaffee
Joshua Chaffee
Enos Clark
Thomas Coleman
Benjamin Colton
Moses Colton
Jonathan Cooley
Rowland Crocker
Samuel Day
Isaac Dunham
Joshua Eddy

Continued on next page

The Lexington Alarm – Cont'd

Benjamin Farnham	Ezekiel Russell
John Hitchcock, 3rd	Reuben Shayler
Joshua Jones	Eleaser Smith
Abel King	John Stearns
Thomas King, Sgt	Calvin Stebbins, Fifer
William King, Lt.	Enos Stebbins, Sgt.
Chileab Merrick	Jesse Warner, Lt.
Samuel F. Merrick	James Warriner, Capt.
Isaac Morris	Ezekiel Wright

Service at Roxbury & Quebec - 1775

Captain Paul Langdon's Co., Col. Danielson's Regt.

- Several memoranda from Paul Langdon to the "Committee of Cloathing at Watertown" appealed for the coats promised the men at their enlistment. These letters were dated from November 27, 1775 to January 19, 1776. Letters from John Langdon while at Roxbury to his wife in July 1775 also mention several Wilbraham men.
- Those indicated below with an asterisk did not enlist into the Massachusetts Army.
- Those with a "Q" were detached for service in Quebec, specified in "A return of Capt. Paul Langdon's Company, in Col. Davidson's Reg^{t} of all the men's names in s^{d} Company, & specifying what town Inlisted from of those dead and of these on Command at Quebeck Oct. 6th 1775."

Benoni Atchinson*
Simeon Bates
Levi Bannister*
Ichabod Beckwith
Eli Beebe
Ezekiel Beebe
David Bliss*
John Bliss, 2d*
Oliver Bliss*
Thomas Bliss*
Josiah Bullard*
Timothy Burr
Aaron Cadwell
Daniel Cadwell, Lt
Levi Cadwell*
Stephen Cadwell*
Daniel Carpenter – Q
John W. Chaffee – Q
Abner Chapin, Jr. - Q
Zebulon Chapin*
Benjamin Chubb – Q
Seth Clark
William Clark
Edward Colton
Frederick Colton
Stephen Crane*
John Davis
Kittridge Davis
Ephraim Dunham
Joseph Dunham
Judah Ely*
Charles Ferry
Lothrop Fuller
Othniel Hitchcock
Silas Hitchcock*
Joseph Hubbard*
James Irving, Jr.*
Joseph Jinnings
John Johnson
Thomas Jones*
Zenas Jones*
John Langdon, Sgt
John W. Langdon*
John Langdon, II
Lewis Langdon*

Continued on next page

Paul Langdon, Capt.
Philip Lyon, Sgt.
Nathaniel Mighets
William Osbon*
Moses Rood
Reuben Shayler
Jonathan Sikes - Q
Nathan Sikes
Daniel Simons
Moses Simons
Ezekiel Squire*
Simon Stacy
Aaron Stebbins, 2nd
Joel Stebbins*
Noah Stebbins*
Daniel Sweetland - Q
Jeriah Sweetland
Phanuel Warner - Q
Samuel Warner, Jr.*
Abner Warriner, Fifer
David Warriner*
Noah Warriner, Sgt.
Seth Washburn
Cyprian Wright
Ephraim Wright
Ephraim Wright, Jr.

Note: Daniel and Jeriah Sweetland were from Somers, Ct They did not march with Captain Langdon on April 20th, but joined him later and did enlist on May 8th. Ephraim Wright and Ephraim Jr. also joined Captain Langdon sometime after April 20th. Neither enlisted.

Service at Ticonderoga – 12/5/76 - 4/2/77

Captain Daniel Cadwell's Co., Col. Timothy Robinson's Detachment

- Following the capture of Fort Ticonderoga by Ethan Allen, Benedict Arnold, and the Green Mountain Boys in 1775, a series of militia companies were called upon to serve as its garrison. Wilbraham provided one of these companies.
- "A Pay roll of Cap[t] Daniel Cadwell's Company in Col[o] Tim[o] Robinson's Detachment of Militia From the State of Massachusetts Pay For Services done the United States of America at Ticonderoga From Dec. 5, 1776 To April 2[d] 1777 Included dated at Springfield May 27th 1777 for the Bounty and two pence a mile More allowed by the State." (180 miles travel. 7 Pounds 7 Shillings bounty. 99 days service. 60 Shillings per month wages.)

Wilbraham's Ticondergoa Garrison:

Joseph Abbott
Stephen Ashley
Benoni Bannister
Moses Barber
Ebeneezer Beebe
Steward Beebe
Zadock Beebe
Sebe Bemont
Thomas Blackmore
Isaac Bliss
Luther Bliss
William Brown
Oliver Burt
Daniel Cadwell, Capt.
Jesse Carpenter
Amos Chaffee
Asa Chaffee
Benoni Chapin
Daniel Chapin
Henry Chapin
Judah Chapin
John Chatterton
Aaron Colton
Edward Colton
Eli Colton
John Colton
Joseph Colton
William Colton, 3d
Justin Cooley
Solomon Cummins
Joel Day
James Edson
Moses Elsworth
Eleazer Fisher
William Fuller
Jabez Hancock
John Hancock
Jeptha Hill
John Hitchcock, 3rd
Perez Hitchcock
William Hitchcock
David Hubbard
Jacob Kindal
James Lamberton

Continued on next page

Service at Ticonderoga – Cont'd

Benoni Clark
Solomon Loomis
John McElwain, Sgt
Robert McMaster, Lt
Judah Moore, Drummer
Isaac Morris
Timothy Murphy
Ebeneezer Oakes
Elijah Palmer
Daniel Parsons, Lt
Joshua Parsons
Jonathan Rogers
Nathaniel Rogers
Timothy Root
Benjamin Russell
Joshua Searles
James Shaw
Jesse Lampear
Knowles Shaw
Luther Smith
Joseph Steal
John Stebbins
Medad Stebbins, Cpl
Moses Stebbins, 3rd
Josiah Tinney
Jonathan Tylar
Samuel Warner, Jr.
Abner Warriner, Cpl
Aaron Waters
Lewis White
Joel Willey
David Wood
Daniel Woodworth
Stephen Wright, Sgt

In December, Captain Cadwell and Sergeant Joseph Abbott died of smallpox at Fort Ticonderoga.

Saratoga & The Bennington Alarm - September 1777

Captain James Shaw's Co, Colonel Charles Pynchon Esquire's Regiment, from 9/24/77 until 10/18/77 for 32 days service.

- "Capt. James Shaw's Company detached for the Reg[t] whereof Charles Pynchon Esq is Col° and ordered to join Gen. Gates army for thirty days Unless sooner Discharged."
- "Each man Entered Sept. 24. Discharged October 18. Miles travelled home 140 - mileage at 1p per mile, 11s 8; Days in service 32 - wages for Continental pay, Capt. £12.16, Lieuts Each £8.12.9, Serjeants £2.10, Privates £2.7."
- The following men served in New York and Vermont at Bennington and near Saratoga:

David Bliss
Gaius Brewer, Sgt
Comfort Chaffee, Sr.
Aaron Chanwell, Cpl
Abner Chapin, Jr., Cpl
Israel Chapin, Lt
John Chatterton
Ebeneezer Colton, Lt
Edward Colton
John Colton
George Cooley
Jabin Cooley
Josiah Cooley, Cpl
Luther Cooley
Judah Ely
Charles Ferry, Sgt
Luther Hitchcock
Phineas Hitchcock
Aaron Howard
Benjamin Howard
Asa Jones
Matthew Keep
Oliver King, Lt
Gad Lamb, Sgt
Jesse Lampear
John Langdon
John Langdon, II
Jonathan Leech
Solomon Loomis
Solomon Lothrop
Jonathan Merrick
Samuel Fiske Merrick
Edward Morris
Isaac Morris
William Osbon
Elijah Parsons
Gordin Percival
Joseph Sexton, Sgt
James Shaw, Capt
Asa Simonds
Joseph Steal
Aaron Stebbins, 2nd
Calvin Stebbins, Fifer
Medad Stebbins, Cpl
Noah Stebbins, Lt
Zadock Stebbins
Daniel Sweetland

Continued on next page

Bennington Alarm Cont'd

Nathaniel Warner
Reuben Warriner
Solomon Warriner
David White
Lemuel Whitney
Judah Willey
David Wood
Timothy Worthington

Captain Joseph Browning's Company, Col. Seth Murray's Regiment

- Lieutenant Colonel Seth Murray, from Hatfield, was a Lieutenant at Lexington and served in various capacities throughout the war, including that of company commander at the Battle of Saratoga in 1777. On July 4, 1780, he was appointed commander of the 2nd Hampshire Regiment. This regiment was raised to reinforce the Continental Army for three months.
- Captain Joseph Browning is credited with various service starting in 1776. He served under Colonel Bliss in 1778. He was "engaged" on July 4, 1780 to lead a company for three months under LTC Murray.
- Note that Joseph Cutt and Caesar Merrick, two of the three black soldiers from Wilbraham, both served in this company.
- All of the men below are credited as serving for the Town of Wilbraham, generally for the period 7/21/80 - 10/10/80 at Suffolk County:

Stephen Bliss
Adam Burdick
Benoni Chapin
John Colton
Luther Cooley
Joseph Cutt
Jesse Elwell
John Goodwill
Asa Hill
Simeon Hitchcock
David Hubbard
James Lamberton
James Langdon
Philip Langdon
Caesar Merrick
Jonathan Sikes
Gaius Stebbins
James Stebbins
Zadock Stebbins
James Thomas
John Thwing
Daniel Warner
Jesse Warner
Francis West

Captain John Carpenter's Guards

- On March 5th, 1779, Captain John Carpenter became the commander of a company guarding stores at Springfield. Commanding mostly a series of 3-months draftees, he served in this capacity through the end of March 1781. On April 1, 1781, Captain Carpenter formed a company of men previously rejected for other service. Although unable to serve in the regular lines, these men were in good enough shape to serve as garrison soldiers at forts. Captain Carpenter served as their commander for about three years and was discharged on March 31st, 1783.
- The following Wilbraham men served at some point under Capt. John Carpenter as guards at Springfield:

Enos Adams
Luther Ainsworth
John Amidon
Benoni Bannister
David Bliss
Jotham Carpenter
Reuben Carpenter
Isaac Chaffee
Isaiah Chaffee, Jr.
Charles Colton
Gideon Colton
John Colton
Nathan Colton
Joel Day
Charles Ferry
James Langdon
Josiah Langdon
Philip Lyon
Chester Morris
Daniel Parsons
James Richardson
Johnson Richardson
Oliver Chapin Sexton
Ethan Smith
Gaius Stebbins
Ebeneezer Thomas
Seth Warner
John Williams
David Wright

Note: Captain John Morgan was also in command of a company of guards for "stores at Springfield and Brookfield." The following Wilbraham men served in this company from January through July 1778:

Benoni Chapin
Abijah Hendrick
James Lamberton
Phineas Newton

Miscellaneous Service

- Enlisted for the Duration of the war: Asa Woodworth May 1777 - June 1783.

- Marched on the Lexington Alarm (April 1775) with other companies:
  Joseph Bumpstead w/Monson
  Peleg Burdick w/Monson
  John Carpenter w/Brimfield
  William Carpenter w/South Brimfield
  Lt. Israel Chapin w/Maj. Andrew Colton
  John Colton w/Maj. Andrew Colton
  Solomon Cummins w/Capt. David Speer
  Joel Day w/Capt. Enoch Chapin
  Gamaliel Dunham w/Monson
  William H. Dunn - Capt. John Crawford
  James Eddy w/Monson
  Matthew Keep w/Maj. Andrew Colton
  Elisha Ladd w/Bolton, CT
  Robert Sessions w/Connecticut
  Joseph Steal w/Maj. Andrew Colton
  Medad Stebbins w/Maj. Andrew Colton

Note: Appendix F of this book contains additional information about each soldier listed in this and the preceding sections. It also contains names for some soldiers that are not easily categorized in these sections but that still should be included as Wilbraham soldiers based on the inclusion criteria given at the start of this book.

IV. Shay's, The War of 1812, and The Militia

Shay's Rebellion

Peace with England did not immediately solve many of the problems facing Wilbraham's citizens. The war had cost an enormous amount of money and, as a result, taxes were very high. Additionally, the paper money the new government had issued was basically worthless ("not worth a Continental") and many people were deep in debt. To illustrate the severity of the money problem, an official state Scale of Depreciation shows that a dollar borrowed on January 1, 1777 was equal to seventy-five dollars at the end of February 1781. A farmer who borrowed a hundred dollars in 1777 would have owed seventy-five hundred in only four years!

Most of western Massachusetts was an agrarian society with mostly subsistence farming. Because of the uncontrolled inflation, very few farmers could afford to pay their debts. As a result, their creditors turned to the debtors courts, thought to be the easiest way to collect debts.

These courts were particularly despised by the farmers, and yeomen from more than 30 towns demanded the abolition or restructuring of these courts. Pressured by their creditors, farmers were frustrated by the mercantile elite and especially their lawyers who, they believed, were "an altogether useless order," blamed for the ruin of "many good, worthy families."

Overt resistance to this situation began in the Hampshire County courts in April, 1782. In July 1782, several Wilbraham militia men were called up to assist the authorities in restoring order following the rescue of the fiery anti-government orator

"I hold it that a little rebellion now and then is a good thing."

Thomas Jefferson in a letter about Shay's Rebellion to James Madsion on January 30, 1787.

Samuel Ely, from the Springfield jail by his supporters. Demonstrations and court closings continued in the area forcing all courts to use soldiers to maintain order by the end of 1786. Rather than work for the changes sought by the people, the state chose aggressive measures to stop the disruptions in the local courts.

Having just gone through a revolution, one might have thought the government might have been more accepting of protest and willing to take popular views into consideration. However, while the leaders of the revolution had fought for political and economic determination, egalitarian social principles were never high on their real agenda.

Even so, it can be argued that Massachusetts was much more tolerant of the farmers dissent than our neighbors. Connecticut, Vermont, and New Hampshire all rapidly put down any trace of impending armed protest. Caught off guard by the first violent action of the farmers on August 29, 1786, officials in Massachusetts initially took no action. In fact, initial attempts to raise the militia to disperse crowds in Worcester in September failed as the troops, many of them farmers themselves and sympathetic to the farmers' plight, refused the call to action. The government then turned to the more commercial areas, such as Springfield, to raise troops.

Daniel Shays moved to Pelham, Massachusetts in 1780 from Hopkinton. He had been a good soldier in the Revolution and rose in rank from sergeant to captain. It is said his commander, General Lafayette, gave him an ornamental sword as a present for his excellent service. A poor man, Shays sold the sword for a few dollars. His fellow officers scorned this ungentlemanly behavior which led eventually to Shays resigning his commission from the army.

The Massachusetts Legislature passed a Riot Act in 1786 authorizing the militia to interrupt assemblies and arrest anyone bearing arms. A frequenter of taverns, the general meeting place for the unhappy farmers, Shays learned that Governor James Bowdoin was to use the militia to guard the Springfield court house. Shays raised a group of men to harass the militia. These armed men took over the Court of Pleas in Springfield on December 26, 1786 and the rebellion was underway.

The Commonwealth mobilized about a thousand men under General William Shepard on January 19, 1787 to deal with this threat to the stability of the government and, of course, to guard the federal arsenal at Springfield. John Langdon, nine Chaffees, and possibly others, according to Mr. Merrick's History of Wilbraham, reported to General Shepard for service. An additional 4,400-man army was also mobilized and waiting in Worcester.

The insurgents planned on a three-pronged attack to defeat General Shepard. The original plan was to attack on January 25th, but a last attempt to convince Shepard to surrender caused a postponement of 24 hours.

Unfortunately, the letter to the Hampshire insurgents in Chicopee and Palmer was intercepted and they proceeded under the old plan.

The government quickly sent another 3,200 troops toward Springfield while Shays moved forward with his 1,100 men to capture the federal armory. Shays quartered his men in Wilbraham as he prepared to take the armory. A very good detailed description of these days is contained in Mr. Merrick's History of Wilbraham.

A meeting of Dr. Samuel F. Merrick, Col. Abel King, and Deputy Sheriff Asaph King of Wilbraham was held and Sheriff King was immediately sent on horseback to warn Shepard of Shays' approach on January 25, 1787. King's warning gave the federal troops ample time to prepare and Shays' troops were turned back after a brief skirmish. Although a few weeks of marches and skirmishes would take place, the showdown at the armory effectively put down any serious threat from Shays and the insurgents. By April, the discharge of the federal troops had begun with the final 200 being released in September 1787.

Less than a dozen men were killed during Shays Rebellion, the nation's first "taxpayer revolt." Almost all of the participants were pardoned and the new country settled itself and moved on. Shays himself moved to upper New York State and died there in 1825.

Although several Wilbraham men served in the militia to put down the rebellion, no specific list of these men has been preserved. The only individual I could identify as having been with Shays was Benjamin Edson. Edson, based on his familiy history, was with Shays at Springfield and was a fugitive in Pelham. Apparently, however, no lasting harm came to Mr. Edson as he and his family continued to prosper very nicely in Wilbraham.

War of 1812

If Massachusetts was the cheerleader for the Revolution, it served an opposite role in the War of 1812. Following the attack on the USS Chesepeake in June 1807, President Jefferson imposed an embargo on trade with the British. In New England, this had the effect of ruining many prosperous shipowners and throwing a number of thriving seaports into a severe economic depression. Rather than toward the British, New England transferred its anger towards Jefferson and his party.

While several of the early battles in the War of 1812 were fought along the New York borders, Massachusetts withheld most of its support for the war and relatively few militia units or soldiers saw service.

A small assembly of troops, including Ensign Robert Sessions and the regimental quartermaster Edward Morris, would be sent to Boston in 1814 for 40 days to defend against an anticipated English invasion but these troops would see no action. This would mark the last time the local enrolled militia would participate in any actual military event.

As best I could determine, the following Wilbraham men served in the War of 1812:

- Ralph Bennett
- Phineas Burr
- Stephen Cadwell, Jr.
- Capt. John Carpenter, Jr.
- Isaac Chapin
- Matthew Cone
- Stephen Cross, Jr.
- Eleazer Hitchcock
- Solomon Jones
- Joel M. Lyman
- Quartermaster Edward Morris
- Nathaniel Knowlton
- Thomas Partridge
- Lt. Robert Sessions, Jr.
- Lt Col. Solomon Warriner, Jr

The Militia

Men obviously continued to serve in the militia in the periods between wars, although the use of the militia was limited to a few men being used here and there to keep order at a trial or a hanging. Following the American Revolution, the local militia units became little more than an excuse for the men to get together once a year and share a few bottles on the training field.

In 1840, the Commonwealth of Massachusetts took over the responsibility for the militia and the towns and cities no longer had their own enrolled militia companies. While this certainly contributed to the military readiness of the Commonwealth, it ended a 200 year old tradition that had served the populace, if not well, then at least well enough.

Rolls for the militia in these "non-war" years are not as well preserved as those for the earlier years. I am told that once the Commonwealth took over, the local towns saw little need to store the old rosters and destroyed many of them. Whether this is the case or not, there seems to be little in the way of records available. From various sources, I have compiled the following scant list of men who served in the militia or in other military service in these later years. Interestingly, most of the names are those of officers:

Jonah Alden, 3rd	-	Ludlow Independent Company (1842)
Amasa Blanchard	-	Fought in the Seminole War
Lorenzo Bliss	-	2LT of North Company in 1837
Isaac Brewer	-	Springfield Artillery, 1837 & 1838
Benjamin Butler	-	Lieutenant Colonel and last commander of the Regiment. Commissioned in 1836.
John Carpenter, Jr.	-	Captain sometime between 1792 and 1812.
Comfort Chaffee, Jr.	-	Captain sometime between 1792 and 1812.
Edward W. Chaffee	-	Springfield Artillery, 1837 & 1838
William Clark	-	Major, no other service information known.
Highland Cleaveland	-	Militia in 1838
Carson K. Cone	-	Adjutant, Commissioned in 1838.
Enoch R. Crocker	-	Colonel, beginning 1838
Benjamin Ellis	-	Militia in 1838, Longmeadow Light Infantry in 1840.
Richard D. Firmin	-	Captain of South Co. 1838-1840.
Levi Flint	-	Captain, no other service information known.
Ephraim Fuller	-	Lieutenant, no other information known.
Peletiah Glover	-	Quartermaster in 1838.
John Hancock	-	First Lieutenant of North Company 1831-1836.
Otis M. Hendrick	-	Major, Commissioned in 1838.
Daniel Knowlton	-	Captain, no other service information known.
Phineas Knowlton	-	Died in the U.S. Navy, October 1827.
Almond Lard	-	1LT of South Co. in 1834.
Joseph Lathrop	-	Captain, no other service information known.
Seth Lathrop	-	Brigade Commander 1831-1833
Jonathan Merrick	-	Lieutenant, no other service information known.

Sidney Moore	-	Springfield Artillery, 1837 & 1838
Philip Morgan	-	Lieutenant, no other service information known.
Edward Morris	-	1st Regiment Quartermaster 1810-1814.
Philip P. Potter	-	Last captain of a Wilbraham militia company.
Charles Sessions	-	Captain sometime between 1792 and 1812.
Oscar Sessions	-	Paymaster, Commissioned 1838
Reuben Sikes	-	Captain of North Company in 1790, Regimental Commander in 1796.
George Stebbins	-	2LT of South Company in 1838.
Jackson W. Stebbins	-	Springfield Artillery, 1837. Was also in Civil War.
Azriel Warner	-	Captain from 1803 – 1805.
James Warriner	-	Captain in 1810.
Marcus Webster	-	No service information.
John West	-	Major, no other service information
Almond Wood	-	Springfield Artillery, 1837
John Work	-	Lieutenant, no other service information known.

The final days of the enrolled militia generally consisted of the yearly Training Day. According to Peck, the training day held each year was a great event. All men between eighteen and fortyfive were required to assemble at certain times, organize into companies, choose officers, and do a certain amount of drilling. Peck further states that, while he wasn't sure how they got their dinner, "New England rum was cheap (abount 60 cents a gallon) and on that day it was plenty and free for every militiaman. The expense was paid by the officers."

Captain Philip P. Potter was the last Captain of the North Company and Captain Richard D. Firmin the last Captain of the South Company. Lt. Colonel Benjamin F. Butler was the last commander of the regiment. They all retained their titles following the militia days and were always referred to as Captain Potter, Captain Firmin, etc.

This then, as sudden as was the ending of the local militia units in 1840, marks the end of this book. I urge you, however, to peruse the appendices. They contain a considerable amount of detail about the individual soldiers and also information that did not particularly fit into any part of the preceding text, but which I felt was important, or at least interesting or smile provoking.

The End

Appendix A – Samuel Warner, Sr's Journal. Kept on the Expedition to Crown Point in 1759.

The journal begins sometime before June 7, 1759.

I now give an acoumpt of our march from Albana to fort Edward. We looded 19 barrils of flower and pork in a battoo and Carrid them within three miles of Stillwarter and there on Looded in the hull of our Regiment there was about 1100 Barrils and then we went to Stillwarters and Looded 25 Barrils in each Battoo which made about 1400 and Carrid them up to about a mile above Sototoga and onloded the Same and then went about one mile and then Looded 22 Barrils which made 1300 and Carrid them to the fott of the falls at fort miller onloded them there the battoos was caried about half a mile and the provision and then Looded againe 20 Barils 1150 and Carrid them to fort Edward this is a trew acount a vary hard voige we had. (Note: Stillwater is more or less midway between Albany and Fort Edward).

This day [June] 7th there was reain Came Before Day and so Held 24 ours carey hard a grat part of the Day and varey Cold Raw weather.

Frey Day 8th Day this Day varey Clowday Raw and Cold in the morning and afterwards more moderate and Sun Shine Varey Cold att Night and just in the morning. We had a vaery grate Larrom by the polesy of the jeneral amhers[t] ordered a party of men att the falls to fier there guns att a marke varey Brisk on purpos to See what Readynes the Armey would Be in the armey was all Drawd up in arms.

Saterday 9th this Day varey Clear and pleasant yesterday and to Day Diging up old Stobs and Rots two feet or three feet over and we moved our tents 40 Rods.

Sabday 10th this Day 6 o clock the hilanders fierd one Round Distinct one after a nither and a fare pleasant Day afterwards our soldiers went to Battooing onley saving the quarter guard and a few that was not well.

Munday the 11th *** one man whipt 400 strips.

Wensday 13th *** there was 240 men Draughted out of our Rijement to Keep the fort edward viz: 19 out of our Company.

Thosday 14th *** This morning there was two rodeisland men Whipt for desart one of them 500 the other 999 this day is the first prayer we heard at Night This day the Revt Mr Forbosh Came into the Camp.

[Then follows a page of entries about letters received and sent]

Saturday 16th this Day there was one of the Conecticots Brought to place of Execution in order to Be shot to Death for Desartion & after giving warning to others and then making a prayer he was placst upon his Knees & his cap over his face Reseved a pardon yesterday and to day we Looded about 300 Batoos and they was carrid to half way Boock and 100 teems.

Sabday 17th there was about a 100 Batoos Carrid from Hear and about 200 other wagins withs tores & about 200 ox teams went from here with stores and the Like making in ye hul 500 ****this Day there was a sermon preacht in ye afternoon By the Rt Mr ferbush text in 15 of Exodus 3 vers the Lord is a man of war the Lord is his Name this was the first sermon that was preacht amongst us. The first Batallun about 200 or three hundred guns [fired] att a mark after sermon there was 3 Rodeisland men whipt for being absent from Role Calling.

Monday 18th *** this morning I was put under gard.

Tusday 19th *** a Cort Marshil upon a young man and Rise & myself to-day for Nothin worth a menshing theyoung man Becas his gun went of upon half Bent and myself Becase I did not goo So quick and Call my sun when Sergeant Daniel Miller Bid me goo I being upon other Duty the same time yet I went Notwothstanding But I had my Dismisshon without any thing more said to me.

Wensday 20th this Day ** the 2nd Recrutes came in from the province of Boston.

Thursday 21st this Day we marcht from fort Edward with about ten Reigements we struck our tents about brake of Day slong our packs about Sun Rise and stood with ym on a full ouer then marcht forward Nor onlooded Nor Rested till we got within five miles of Lake gorge there Rested about one ouer and half varey hot men allmost Beet out By going without vittuals in the morning about 500 teems and wagins the officers had no packs the genral and other big officers had horsis and servens they did not Consider the poor solders Had they Had any Compashoon upon poore Solders they wood not a dun as they Did one man Dyed by Reson of Such Hard traveling and Drinking of warter this was a Conectucut man and two or three more said they ware a Dying the armey was marcht of in the morning on a sudden and had not time to git any Refreshment to Carey with them But God in His providence has spared men's Lives & Carrid threw hather to *we shall not dey Before our time*

Freyday 22d this Day in the morning fare and plesent grate dele of gaiming and Feeterge [performing of feats] tho a grate Complaint among the solders By Reason of there hardships the Day before

Sabday 17th there was a flagg of truse Came in to half way Bruck to see whether we had any prreasners to Exchang

Saterday 23d ** Varey Hot * thunder * no Rain. A Cort Mashil to Day upon a soldir for as tis soposed for Steeling of a Hatchit he is judged to Be whipt 50 Lashis which he Had -- a grate Number of wagins came in to Day 150 or 200

Tuesday 26. ** thisDay order Came out in general that No solder should Drink any warter without it Being Boild Except he had ginger in it.

Wensday 27 ** Benoney atchinson and Isaac Whittemore Come here to Day.

Thosday 28 *** this Day I Entered into bisnes of a mason two Regements fiered plattwoons.

Saterday 30th *** Coll. Whitens [Whiting's] Regiment marcht here to Day tis said they are gon to Mohawke River in for german flats the wagins and teems Came in this Day from the french

Munday 2d ** about ten o'clcok in the morning a partey of about 60 of the inemy fell on a party of the gersey Blew and Kild 8 and scalpt them upon the Spot and wounded 3 more this was in fill view of our armey a more protickular a compt there was 18 of the garsey blew went to git Bare one the North of our Camps and thare it was soposed about three or five score of the inemy got Between our men and the gard and which Kild and wounded and tuck all But one they were followed by Rogers about tem miles and then they tuvk to there Batoos the account was there was 11 batoos and 20 od in each as they thought by the No.

Teusday 3d ** There was four Brase 18 pounders or 22 Brought in to Day Sum small pesses the 2d Recruts from Boston and harford Came in to Day -- Capt Jacob with 30 men went out to day to find the inemy if could find any 24 more was dug up out of one hole whare we did Build the fort four Iron guns 22 pounders Came in and afterwards two more Brase guns in the Hole making 10 22 or 24 pounders and 12 twelve pounders

Wensday 4th ** 24 more Dug up in one hole two french Desarters came in to Day

Thusady 5th. *** alarum att Night By ye Reson of an indians fiering on one of the senterey and he Riturned a Shoot again and woonded him By the Sine of Blood thare is a fort a Reacted the North end of Element Hill.

Saturday 7th I went about the Element Hill on the North End of it there is a fort of 14 squares or turns in it made with wood and stoane and a horpottal of Stoane the Length about 8 Roods the wedth about Eighteen feet from out side to out side the thickness of the Wale two feet and 1/2 the hith about five feet. Sabday 8th ** three men Belonging to Coll Witeens Rimt Dyed in one Horspiteetel this Day was a Varey grate Day of Blooing of Rocks.

Munday 9th ** We have News of genl Woolfs takeing of some strong place up Canaday River this Day there came in a party of the Indions under the command of Capt Jacob that went Down the Lake sum Days ago tis said the Indias fel on him & wounded ye Capt and another of his men. I tuck more observation of Building an in sted of one Hospotitel there is three more all in a few Roods of one a nither one stoon two wood housen

Tuesday 10th ** one man Capt of the waginers was convicted of Steeling the Kinds tools was Judged by a Cort Marshil to be whipt 36 Lashis att the hed of Every Regiment which he had ***

Thursday 12. This Day By Brake of Day there was about 600 men set out to goo Down the Lake about 8 o clock in the morning they came to a party of french and Indins Jes upon the first Narrows and a small iggagement it seemed to bee by what we coold see the grate guns played they drove the Indions of -- this day their was five Barrils of Rum and two of goine stove in a few Rods where I was at work selling contrary to order.

Fryday 13. This day we was Draughted out which is the 3d time I have Ben pitcht upon for this work of mason -- at noon a man shot to Death for Desertion

Saterday 14 at Night our first Batallun and Lymans Regt and some others came to Jine the armey.

Wensday 18th Wim Hancock and Abner Parsons Came up to day

Thusday 19th one man whipt for strikeing an officer at the head of every Rigement a post came in to day Being an account of a small fort was beset by the Inemy our men took and kild a great Number of ym

Freyday 20th one man shot to Death for steeling

Saterday 21st this day the armey marcht for ticonderoga they struck there tents about three o'clock in the morning and about sun rise the Bigest part of the armey got to the warter side they Borded three Batoos about Sun an ouer and half high and set of about twelve o clock they ware out of sight and they cep a going of all the Day afterwards 10-20-30 Batoos at a time till sun one ouer and 1/2 high att night then the Sloop set sail and att Sun Down she was about 15 miles of tis soposed to be 12000 men 15 morters 12. 12 pounders 6. 24 pounders of Brase 3 18 pounders of Iron & a grate number of swivels this Day there is a'grate morning among the Wiming as if they had Lost there husborns **

Sabday 22d there is 400 Men Came in to Day 100 of them gone Down the Lake or 200 there is 62 masons left behind there is 150 or 200 in the hospititel

Wensday 25th this morning about Day the grate Boot came in ** and Brought the News that we our armey ware well intrencht where the french had theres Last year and played there cannon upon them and also we had taken 2 Indins and Kild 2 and taken 4 french and Kild two with the Lose of one man

Hampshire Regiment is come to the Lake in order to goo to Oswago News came in that Magr Rogers had a grate fite Between tyconderoga and Crown point. A Large guneylow or two mast Boot went of with about 90 or a 100 horsis to tyconderoga

Freyday 27th I heard a man say that was there that a minester Kep Count of the French Cannon that was fired Wensday night the No is 150 and our men had not fiered any then worth menchurning

Saturday 28th in the morning Coll fitch Came in with his Rigement ** our interpreter said that *** there was but 200 men in the fort and 300 in crown point fort and said our men might take it without fiering a gun and said that Rogers had Kild and sunk 500 of there men in Shamplain Lake. *** ye french fiered sum hundreds of Cannon and Burns the Day and Night Before they left the fort they fiered the magascen & lew up what they coold the night before Last *** this day two Bond fiers made one the a count of tyconderogas Being taken.

Thusday [August] 2d this day 12 o cloock news came that crown point was Blown up By the french the truth I will wait for

Esq Woodbridge says it is trew without fail and the french are a fortifying about ten or 15 miles Beyond

Saterday 4th I had the news that our Battallun marcht to crown point this day

Sabday 5th a tumult among the setlers ye officer tuck there Rum and Brandey from them

Teusday 7th By the Reson of the Heat the Injineare and two or three more were Carid from thare work to share tents and I ware varey much put to it to keep upon my Leegs

Saterday 11th There was an Express come here & went over the Lake and he said he had the news of an officer he saw a Leater opened & which gave an a count that genl woulf had got well intrincht clost By Queback without the Loss of any men as to the truth I will Leave att present

Tusday 16th No news onley the a count of a former storey of a man shot down a Reaven and she spake

Saterday 18th heard of Janerll Jonsons sending in 627 Captives to albana and he Distroayed 500 more

Sabday 19th Let Howard told me that he had Bin to crown point and he was informed there that there ware orders for 115000 sticks of timber 30 feet long and 15 inches thick sd timber to Be Brought as fast and Can Be hewed one three Sides and that they ware Blooing up Rocks 7 feet deep

Munday 3d [September] Rain the bigest part of the day and ye coll said Dam it you shall work so we Did

Freyday 7th an express came in to Day about janll Woolfs being Defeated and Drove back one leter I sent to Daniel Warner and one to Sister Lois moved into my new tent.

Saterday 15th about one o clock had orders to march to crown point and about dark I sot of for the same with 30 men

Sabday 16th morning we landed att tyconde Roga Before Sun Rise and then marcht Right of to crown point and got there Sun two ours high

Tuesday 18th began to work att crown point

Freyday 21st begun the stone Barrack

Wensday 26 I was sick and could not work

Wensday 10th [October] Lt Hutchins Came here Last Night and gave an account of genirel Woolfs destroying of Quebeck

Thusday 11th one Coullee a captive gave an a Count of Mr. Williams sister in Canada and one Sargent Couen was taken when Hitchcock was killed. 5500 men set off from here for St. Johns.

Saterday 13th one Drove of fat oxen Came in from No fore -- this night news came in from the armey that in a fogg a good part of our armey got By two french Sloops Before proseved them amediately our armey Landed one Boath sids Before an reft of the french But 19th of ye Lite Enfanty went to the french Soposein they ware our own sloops and ware taken Sd french are Blockt up Near Orter Crick

Teusday 16 I have a Reumer of an express that is gone to our genirel yt moon calm and gell woolf is Kild and there armies most all Destroyed one Boath sides By a fare field fight But we got the victory But as to the truth I leave at present 32000 french 16000 of ours

Wendsay 17th News cam By an express from our genll woolfs armey that they Drove into the french trench at by that means got the victory with the loss of ye generll and 400 men & Kild mont Calm & 1600 men

Thosday 18. News that the Armey two french Sloop and sunk the other and the Brigg get Cleere this Day

Freyday 19th I heard of the Death of William Harris be Dyed Last Tuesday 16th of this month -- Last night there came in an

Indin Captive and gave a Count of Capt Canada Being Kild and his men after taken and Capt Jacob & others Capt Jacobs is in gail

Sabday 21st there came in 2000 Regulars, which is part of the armey.

Freyday 26th there went about two hundred men to make the Rode goo to No four

Munday 29th Aaron Prest Dyed

Wensday 31. Varey cold the ground frose and Ise half an Inch thick in the morning to day our Drum (?) bill Brocks Dyed

Thosday 1st [November] Last Night a Number of men under gard for tempting to goo hum and to Day a Member of the garsey Blews under gard but Dismist to Day

Teusday 6th the Solders Came from fort Edward here to Day

Wensday 17 News Came in to Day that Rogers had Distroyed St. francy way without the Loss of any man But 12 wounded

Sabday 25th [17 Days lost of the Journal] ground frose hard We marched to Davises fort and campt there.

Munday 26th cold and Snow and hold to while Noon then Rain We marched to Northfield and Lay there Capt putnam of Rode Island Dyed att -------

Teusday 27th Cold Rainy Day I marcht from Northfield to Sunderland I logged at Carsons Warner's

Wensday 28th This Day fare and plesant morning -- and south winds varey raw after wards I went from Sunderland to my one hous this day.

Appendix B Colonial Soldiers of Wilbraham

Town	Name / DOB	Rank / DOD	Age	Cemetery
--	**Alvord, Aaron**	Sgt		

Also Alvard. Pvt in Nov 1754. Marched on the Lexington Alarm of 4/20/75. Served 10 days.

Town	Name / DOB	Rank / DOD	Age	Cemetery
Wilb.	**Atchinson, Benoni**	Pvt		
	-	12/6/1786	81	

Lived at 720 Stony Hill Rd. Family owned 687 Stony Hill as well.

Town	Name / DOB	Rank / DOD	Age	Cemetery
--	**Ball, Jonathan**	Major		
	-	3/7/1760		

Died of smallpox in Wilbraham. Served at Louisburg.

Town	Name / DOB	Rank / DOD	Age	Cemetery
--	**Bartlett, Moses**	Cpl		
	-	11/5/1774	63	Adams
--	**Bliss, Aaron**	Cpl		
	-	1776		

Part of military expedition to Hatfield in August 1748 for 58 days under Capt. Isaac Colton. Served at Crown Point under Capt. Luke Hitchcock from 5/5/1755 to 10/1/1755. Died in 1776 as part of Army of Canada.

Town	Name / DOB	Rank / DOD	Age	Cemetery
Wilb.	**Bliss, Abel**	Ensign		
	1706	4/30/1762	54	Adams

One ref as officer prior to 1754. Became Ensign in 1756. Was 46 in July 54 muster. In Church Records, 1760. Home at 182 Mountain Rd, Wilb.

Town	Name / DOB	Rank / DOD	Age	Cemetery
Hamp.	**Bliss, John, 2d**	Colonel		
	1727	11/3/1809	83	Hampden

Moved from Longmeadow in 1750 to 128 Somers Rd, Hampden. In 1763 owned 142 South Rd.

Town	Name / DOB	Rank / DOD	Age	Cemetery
Wilb.	**Bliss, Stephen**	Pvt		
Wilb.	**Burt, Moses**	Captain		
	--	7/28/1786	77	Adams

Church records 1760 as Sgt. There are 2 Moses Burt's in Adams, 1 w/no rank. Owned a sandstone quarry near Mile Tree School.

Long-Meadow? **Burt, Nathaniel** Lt
- 9/8/1755 45
Killed in battle with Dieskau (Lake George). Also claimed by Longmeadow and may be buried there according to Copeland (Hist. Of Hampden County).

Wilb. **Cadwell, Daniel** Captain
1733 1777 44
Sgt in Nov. 1754. Church records in 1760 as a sergeant. Lived on Ridge Rd in Wilbraham. Served at Crown Point under Capt. Luke Hitchcock from 4/11/1755 to 10/1/1755. See Revolutionary War records. Died of smallpox in 1777.

Wilb. **Cadwell, Ebeneezer** Lt
1737 Btwn 1810-20
4th Gr. Granddaughter in NH has his powder horn with his name made at Fort Edward in 1758. Born in Springfield.

Hampden **Chaffee, Joseph, Jr.**
- 3/15/1760 59 Hampden
Died of smallpox. Lived at 48 Stafford Rd, Hampden, before 1760.

-- **Coates, ?** Captain
- 1/4/1757
Possibly this is David Coates from Essex County. Wilbraham Vital Records shows only an F&I soldier named "Coates" dying in Wilbraham.

Palmer **Colton, Isaac, Sr.** Captain
Originally from Harvard. In the company called for Louisburg in 1745 but that built Fort Massachusetts instead. Captain in August 1748 on 58 day expedition to Hatfield. Corporal in Nov. 1754. From April 11th to Nov. 27th, 1755, as a resident of Springfield, he served in Luke Hitchcock;s Co. in the Crown Point Expedition. In August 1761, he was an Ensign in Col. Richard Saltonstall's Regiment (4/18 - 12/2 in Capt. James Gray's Company). From March 4th to November 10, 1762, he was a Lieutenant, according to a list with LTC Joseph Goldthwait's name at the top. On March 2, 1763, he was a Lieutenant in Captain Jonathan Carver's Company. He served as a Captain in Col. Brewer's Regt at Roxbury in Revolution, commissioned 6/17/75.

-- **Colton, Isaac, 3rd**
- 4/12/1756 26 Adams (Mem.)
Died at Ft. Edward sometime after June 1759 according to gravestone but Adams Tour book and "Wilbraham Vital Statistics" say 1756 at age 26.

Hampden **Davis, John**
- 2/251826 - Hampden
Lived at 48 Stafford Rd, Hampden, in 1761.

-- **Day, Samuel** Captain
- 1771
Served at Ft. Massachusetts May 27 & 28 1747 under Col. John Stoddard. Green Mountain Patrols in 1749. LT in 1749, Was Cpt in August 1754 at age 56 until died in 1771.

-- **Dunham, Thomas** Pvt
No information other than that he served.

-- **Hitchcock, Gideon**
- 3/13/1758 - Adams
Not sure of service. Gravestone says he was "slain by ye enemy Mar. 13, 1758."

Hampden **Hitchcock, John, 3rd** Lt
4/21/1722 1807
Served on Western Frontier of Mass. 9/2-9/12/1754 under Capt. Isaac Colton. Lived at 300 Wilbraham Rd in 1742 with father Luke. See Revolutionary War records. Born in Springfield, died in Wilbraham.

-- **Hitchcock, Paul** Pvt
Served in Capt. Daniel Burt's Company in 1758.

Hampden **Hitchcock, Reuben**
Replacement for Louisburg Army 6/23/1745. Died in epidemic in the service.

-- **Jones, John**
-- 1757 21 Adams
At Quebec in 1757 according to Copeland's History of Hampden County. Memorial stone in Adams Cemetery says he died at Quebec in 1757.

Wilb. **Jones, Thomas**
1739 2/14/1825 86 Adams
Town "legend" is that Lt. Thomas Jones, an F&I War veteran, built the house at 200 Main St. in 1755. However, Thomas Jones would have only been 16 in 1755. There was an Ensign Thomas Jones at Louisburg in 1745 -- could this have been his father? Perhaps we have credited Thomas, Jr. with his father's exploits?

Hampden **King, William, Jr.** 1Lt
1724
William Jr. in F&I War at Crown Point in Oct. 1755 under Capt. Samuel Miller. Church records as Sgt in 1760. Born in Palmer.

Hampden **Langdon, John**
6/1/1728 10/10/1822 94 Hampden
Crown Point 1755. Son of Lt. Paul Langdon.

Hampden **Langdon, Paul**
12/16/1725 6/23/1804 79 Hampden
Son of Lt Paul Langdon. He was a "Centinel" in 1747 and 1748 under Lt. John Catlin and also under Major Israel Williams. He was in Captain Samuel Day's Company around 1756. From April 19 to December 9, 1755, he was a sergeant in Capt. Luke Hitchcock's Company, Col. John Worthington's Regiment, serving in the Crown Point Expedition.

Hampden **Langdon, Paul** Lt
9/12/1693 12/3/1761 69 Hampden
Served at Ft Massachusetts 5/19-6/10/1747 under Col. Ephraim Williams and at Fort Shirley 12/10/1747-5/18/1748 and again 6/11-10/31/1748 under Lt. John Catlin. Sergeant from Nov 1754-1771. Church records of 1760 say he was Lt then. Came to Hampden in 1741 to 229 Somers Rd. Also owned 263 Scantic Rd prior to 1765. Previously lived in Salem, Hopkinton, and Union. Land passed to son Paul the grandson John.

Wilb. **Lyon, Philip** Sgt
1729 1811 — (d. Ludlow)
Also, see Revolutionary War records. Born in Woodstock, VT, died in Ludlow.

Wilb. **Merrick, Thomas** Lt
- 2/20/1785 82 Adams
Was Ensign in March 1749. Green Mountain Patrols in 1749. LT at age 51 in August 1754 at least thru 1771. Town Moderator in 1770. Son of Capt. John Merrick.

-- **Mygate, George**
Replacement for Louisburg Army at Cape Breton, 6/23/1745. Died in epidemic there.

-- **Newton, Phineas** Lt
- 7/12/1779 71
No information about military service. Died in Wilbraham.

-- **Parsons, Aaron** Pvt
2/14/1737
No information about military service.

Wilb. **Shaw, James** 2Lt
Louisburg Exped to Cape Breton, 6/23/1745. Green Mountain Patrols in 1749. Sgt at Louisburg in 1745 in 10th Co, 9th Regt. 2Lt in Provincial Arty Co. of 1st Regt. Home at 383 Mountain Rd.

Wilb. **Sikes, Nathaniel**
1728 1760 32 Adams
Died at Fort Edward. Also listed as being from Monson.

Hampden **Stebbins, Aaron** Sgt
2/20/1715 1/22/1789 74 Adams
Lived at 16 Somers Rd.

Wilb. **Warner, Jesse** Lt
10/15/1738 2/20/1784 46 Adams
See Revolutionary War records.

Wilb. **Warner, Samuel, Jr.**
1/1/1734 12/14/1823 89 Adams
Son of Samuel, Sr. See Revolutionary War records.

Wilb. **Warner, Samuel, Sr.**
10/3/1708 9/10/1783 75 Adams
Home was at 859 Stony Hill Rd.

-- **Warriner, Aaron** Pvt
- 12/13/1762

-- **Warriner, Benjamin** Pvt
1698 1/22/1764 66 Adams
Crown Point under Capt. Luke Hitchcock 4/11/1755 - 10/1/1755. Brother of Moses.

Wilb. **Warriner, James** Captain
1725 6/29/1795 70 Adams
F&I War. Nov. 1754. Possibly born 1723, died 1793. Born in Springfield. Replacement for Louisburg Army 6/23/1745. Ensign in July 1774. Town Clerk 1773-78, 1781-85. Captain of Lexington men.

Wilb. **Warriner, Moses** Pvt
1708 3/20/1766 58 Adams
See Revolutionary War records.

-- **Wright, Benjamin** Pvt
2/8/1747

-- **Wright, Timothy** Pvt
Served at Ft #4 9/11/1754-2/26/1755 under Capt Wm. Williams.Crown Point 1755

Appendix C – Dr. Samuel F. Merrick's Journal of his service Northward – 1776

Dr. Samuel Fiske Merrick, son of Reverend Noah Merrick, the first minister of a Protestant church in Wilbraham, Massachusetts, received his M. D. degree after studying with Dr. Brainard of Haddam, Connecticut. A surgeon's mate in Col. Elisha Porter's regiment that went to reinforce the Northern Army then besieging Quebec. The doctor was in the disastrous retreat from Canada and helped care for the many soldiers ill with smallpox or diarrhea.

Dr. Merrick left home on April 22, 1776 and began writing in his journal on May 1st. His journal ends on September 16th. The first three pages of the journal, it is said, were almost completely destroyed, so the first readable entry begins with 11 May 1776, when his section of the Army was moving on Lake Champlain to reinforce the troops of the Northern Army then in the region of Quebec.

The Journal:

11 May. Rested comfortably last night on straw bed. Early in the morning we proceeded without much wind felt. Toward evening there came up a gale of wind which obliged us to land on the Westernshore in a bay about four miles to the Northward of the four brothers, so called, where we encamped in thin woods, spread a table in the wilderness, eat heartily, and laid down to sleep.

12 Sunday. In the morning the wind being NW we lay bye till after twelve when the wind abating we set out and rowed about twelve miles, night coming on, encamping again in the woods.

13. Early in the morning, the wind being in the South, we hoisted sail a little after sun rise and sailed at a fine rate. Arrived at St. Johns [St. Jean] before night. Heard very unfavorable news from Quebec. No prospect of a house to lodge in this night.

14. Lodged in a Batteau last night. In the morning set out for Chamblee (1). Came very near being carried over the Falls by the ignorance or malace of the pilot but luckily preserved. Arrived at Chamblee about 10 miles from St. Johns after nine oclock where we waited to bake bread all day. In the evening went to a French house to lodge.

15. Lodged in a French house last night. In the morning set out for Sorell with a fine wind, made no stop until we arrived there a little after five PM where we found the Regiment in camp having the Small Pox. .... everything wearing a gloomy aspect. Expect the enemy upon us soon. The company greatly exposed to Small Pox. About sun set pitched our tents in the field, soon after lay down for sleep in a tent.

16. Slept well last night in a tent for the first time. In the morning introduced to Dr. [Abraham] Watson. Dined with Col. [Elisha] Porter. Spent the afternoon in the field. Toward night moved our tents to the place of parade, pitched them early in the evening, went to bed on the ground with Capt. Chapin.

17. Taried in the Camp till about eleven then went three miles up the river with Dr. Watson to visit those sick with Small Pox. In the after noon returned to the camp. Received orders to inoculate the Regiment, which we were infecting with all dispatch when counter order came and forbid upon pain of death.

18 May 1776 Saturday. Taried in camp all day. In the after noon all those that were inoculated yesterday were ordered to Montreal tomorrow morning.

19 Sunday. A little before ten in the morning went three miles to visit those sick with the Small Pox. Visited upwards of fifty and returned at night. This day accidentally fell upon my old friend Samuel Fiske. What will be come of me God only knows. No flesh at all in the stors and but a trifle of flour, scarse any powder & but a little ammunition.

20. This morning all those that were inoculated set out for Montreal. Mr. Fiske concluded to tent with me. No flesh at all

dealt out for two mornings past. Men refuse to go upon duty, for the want of provision. Great numbers deserted last night. 21 Tuesday. This morning received intelligence that 4,000 Hessians & Hanoverians are a little off from Boston, 10,000 more gone to New York, that Col. Beetles' Regiment to the westward was defeated & Capt. Bliss of Concord was taken, both which accounts are said to be brought by express. Last night a few barrels of Pork arrived & brought an account that 150 more are arrived at St. Johns and may be expected soon, which puts a new face on the Army. Last night Maj. General Thomas broke out with the Small Pox & this day sat out for Chamblee. Brigadier General Thompson takes command till Gen. Wooster arrives from Montreal. It is said orders will be given to go soon.

22 Wednesday. Tarried in the camp in the forenoon. In the after noon walked out three miles to visit the sick when word came that orders were given to march with dispatch to St. Johns. Immediately went down to camp and prepared for the march, which we were ordered to early in the morning.

23 Thursday: Set out early in the morning for St. Johns & proceeded about one and twenty miles to Capt. Jacobs in Sandmill.

24 Friday: In the morning proceeded on our march, the wind against us. At night put up at a Frenchman's house. Travelled all day afoot. 15 miles this day.

25 Saturday: The wind very strong against us so that we arrived at Chamblee but a little before night. Pitched our tents. Col. Porter takes the command. 9 miles this day.

26 Sunday: Early in the morning went to visit the sick, all day among them. Greatly worried.

27 Monday. Awoke in the morning much out of health, spent most of the day in my tent, at night a little better. This evening Leut. Luke Day arrived, when I received a letter from Brother Pliny, which put joy in my heart.

28. Unwell all day. Things wear a most dismal aspect. What will be the event of all, God only knows.

29. This morning no better. Took a vomit which operated tolerably well, after which drank a dish of tea. Felt much better. In the afternoon went to my usual employment, exceeding cold this day for the season.

30 Thursday. Almost recovered my health. This morning a grand Council of War sat consisting of the following General Officers, viz. [David] Wooster, [Benedict] Arnold, [Frederick] Woldtke and all the Field Officers that could well be collected. Nothing transpired as yet 5 cl PM, except Leut. Hunts being ordered to Montreal with all dispatch. Some conjecture that with ye troops that way we to be recalled, others that only those of Col. Porter's Regiment which have the Small Pox, but which is the most agreeable to truth time will discover. This I believe is certain that unless some material alternative takes place in consequences of the council, great part of the Officers as well as Soldiers will desert their colours.

31 Friday. Last night the Council broke up & this morning the members returned to their several destinations. In the Evening orders were given for every man to lv upon his arms & to stand ready for a moments warning.

June 1 Saturday. No alarm last night. It seems by the appearance of things that we are to leave this place soon as great preparation is making for removing the Cannon & Ordnance stores. All the men fit for duty are ordered to go upon fatigue to morrow morning, necessary guards only excepted. The move next seems to be towards St. Johns.

June 2 Sunday. About sun rise this morning departed this life and in the after noon was decently interd with the honours of war the Hon. Major General [John] Thomas who presided as Chief in this department, a man in whom we put great confidence & his death is esteemid as a great loss to America in general but particularly to this department under our present circumstances. About twelve clock at noon, past through this place, General Sullivan 10 from St. Johns & I suppose is gone to Montreal. Expect he will take the command in this district. Stors, Baugage &c constantly arriving from Sorrell.

3 Monday. This day past through this place General [John] Sullivans Brigade, for Sorrell. Col. Porter orderd all those of his Regiment fit for duty to be in readiness to embark for the same place tomorrow but Im inclind to think we shall not go till the next day. Suppose I shall go with them.

4 Tuesday. Dr. Watson arives from St Johns and concludes to proceed forward with the Regiment & leave me to take care of the sick here & at St John. To set sail tomorrow morning.

5. About one clock PM the regiment set sail for Sorrell. What will be the event of the movement God only knows but when the whole army is collected it will make one so formidable that I hope the enemy will flee before them.

6. This day receivd intelligence that the enemy was above the three Rivers marching by and very strong. An express arrived for amunition and all the men fit for duty, who are preparing to push forward with full haste. The enemy I fear will be too strong for us. If so and they succeed now, the ground will not be regained for many a day.

7. This morning sat out for St Johns to Visit the sick there and on the road. Arivd there before night. Found the company in better circumstances than was represented. Tis reported that General Washington is on the road for this department but wants confirmation.

8 Saturday. Tarried with the company all day in expectation of getting medicines of Dr. [Samuel] Stringer but much disappointed. The news of the day is that the Enemy are repulsed with great loss at a little distance from Sorrell but the particulars we have not heard.

9 Sunday. About twelve sat out with Leut S Day for Chimbly. Arrived there in time of Divine Service performed by Mr. Avery Chaplain of Col [John Peterson] Patisons Regiment. Heard but part of the Sermon, which is the only part of one I have heard

since I left my Fathers house. Sabaths here are almost forgot. May I never forget them. The news of yesterday contradicted.
10. Awoke in the much [morning] unwell, not able to visit the sick all day. Felt no better at night. Nothing material hapning this day.

11 Tuesday. Recovered my health tolerably well. Nothing material.

12. This day Mr. Beeman arived from Sorell & brought an account that General [William] Thompson was defeated at the 3 rivers with the loss of about 50 men & he himself was not heard of, supposed to have been kild. [General Thompson was captured, not killed.]

13. Fell in company with Col Baldwin who gave me a glass of Cyder, a mighty rarity here.

14 Friday. This morning Mr. Spring Chapin who was in the defeat near Trois Rivers arived here from Sorrell and gave a particular account of the affair. He says that there was not more than twenty kild. General Thomson, two Col Evans, Mr. McAuly, chaplain, & Dr. Bennet with four others were taken Prisoners. The enemy he says are very strong. They ride triumphant where ever they go (in the department) & I verily believe they will till they get to Crown Point, and unless some more particular attention is paid towards regulating affairs the day is their own.

15. Early in the morning a report was spread that the army was retreating from Sorell which was soon confirmed by the batteries which arived from there. The whole attention of the garison was turnd imediately towards removing all the public stors together with the sick. Towards night came myself up to the head of the falls about 1-1/2 miles where I lodged.

16 Sunday. In the morning marched for St. John in company with Mr. Avery & Mr. Breck, arived there about eleven, waited for the sick in the Batteaus to come up which they did about four, & near Sun set sat out for Isle aux Noix.(2) The men that were well greatly woried so that I was oblidged to row myself

great part of the way. We arived there after two in the morning in the most dismal circumstances. Nothing but the Canopy of Heaven to cover us. Some of the men not able to stand alone, but the Lord is our keeper. Why should we fear?

17. Slept about an hour and half in the open air. Awoke in the morning. Walk round to see the situation of things. Found the People in the most deplorable circumstances I ever beheld. Great numbers living in distress & some breathing their last. Great part in the open air and nothing that is comfortable to give them. Myself in comfortable health. What an inestimable blessing it is. The Lord grant that I may walk worthy of so great a favour. Four died last night and this morning the sick constantly coming from St Johns. At night heard that an Oficer was fired upon between Chamblee and St Johns, suppose by the Indians or Canadians.

18. Taried at Isle aux Noix all day. Heard that Fort Chamblee was burnt & our army on their march yesterday for St Johns. At night reported that the barracks at St Johns was burnt and the army set out for this place.

19. Last night the army arived here from St John. In the morning the Island was full of men. In the after noon Order was issued for the sick to go immediately to Crown Point but it was so late before they could get ready that they conclude to set off in the morning. I am Ordered to go with them.

20. About twelve went aboard for Crown Point. Very little wind. Rowed upwards of twenty miles to an Isleland called the Isle of Mott [Isle au Motte] six miles to the southward of the white House so caled where we landed & encamped for the night.

21. In the morning waited for the Batteaus to come up. About eight clock the three that lay behind arived. Found that Ensign Stiles of Capt Shephards Company was dead. We soon interd his body in as decent a manner as we could & proceeded on our way half after nine. But a trifle of wind. Rowed till sun about an hour high when we landed in order for lodging. Uncertain how far this day.

22. Early in the morning proceeded on our way. Soon fell in company with Leut Col Read & - Child who piloted us to Mr. Giltilands two & thirty miles from Crown Point. Treated with great hospitality by him. Eat a fine Venison stake & lay down in a tent for sleep.

23. Sunday. In the morning went to Mr. Giltiland. Drank a dish of Tea. The wind being south concluded to tarry all day. At noon invited to dine on a fine piece of rosted venison which we did. This put new life into us having had no fresh provision for a considerable time, tho a little unwell myself which was the rather unfortunate as such entertainments are but rare.

24. A little after Eleven we set out, the wind against us. Rowed in about six miles of Crown Point, went ashore to one Averys an inholder, here we lodged.

25. Last night there was an alarm. A report propagated that the Indians had fired upon our men on the western shore, by reason whereof numbers sat off in the night but we thought it proper to take our rest till morning, which we did. When we arose drank a dish of Chocolat. Waited till near ten for Col. [Philip] Williams to come up, when we sat out without him. Soon arived at Crown Point where we found him. Pitched our tent on a fine parade. Heard that a whole Boats crew of southern troops was cut off by the Indians.

26 Wednesday. Taried in camp all day, nothing material hapning.

27. This day being at liesure viewed deliberately the ruins of the old Fort. It apears to have been an exceeding strong fortification before it was destroyd by fire.

28 Friday. This morning after five clock died Phanuel Warner [from Wilbraham] of the Small Pox. In the after noon there was an alarm, a report that the Indians bad done damage to the inhabitants. A party of men was immediately sent across the bay to the west shore where they found the Indians had taken one prisoner & done some trifle other damage.

29 Saturday. This day Joseph Sykes Jr arived here from New England and brought sundry letters for myself from my friends.
30 Sunday. Nothing material hapning this day. Expecting the Troops from the Northward every hour.

July 1 —

2. Last night about twelve clock the army arived from the Isle aux noix & this morning they encamped.

3. This day wrote a letter to my Father. Nothing material hapning this day. The army is very sick at present. Those that were left well at Isle aux Noix are great numbers now unwell.

4. The general orderd partys to be sent to the Onion river & Cumberland head.

5. This morning three soldiers belonging to the southward receivd twice thirty nine stripes apeice for at night. General Skyler [Philip John Schuyler] & General [Horatio] Gates arived here and it is thought it will be a grievance to General Sullivan to have the comand taken from him.

6 Saturday. This day orders were issued for the sick to be reviewed by the Director General in order to be sent off, where is uncertain. Some said to Fort George, others not.

7 Sunday. Attended public worship this day. Heard Mr. Breck preach for the first time. In the afternoon Orders were issued for removing all the artilery & artilery stors aboard the boats which is an order very unexpected about which there is various opinion. Some say to the northward, others to the southward & I am inclined to think the latter is the most probable, which order I doubt not will be much against the minds of the Oficers of the New England forces if not of those of the southward. Let it be which way it will

8. This day the Commander Mr Skyler aquainted the army in general Orders that General Sullivan was agoing to General Washington at New York and I hear he is to go to morrow.

9. The topick of conversation yesterday and to day is which way the army is to go but they generally agree now that we are for the southward. In the evening had some uncomfortable words with Ensign Snow ariseing principally if not wholely from my smoking tobacco, the first Oficer with whom the like has hapned since I have been in the service.

10 Wednesday. In the morning receivd orders from Col Porter to be in readiness to go to Fort George with the sick which I conclude to comply with, tho contrary to my inclination, & about two oclock PM we sat out. We were forbid to land on the east side of the lake or at Ticonderoga which put us to a considerable trouble for we found no place where we could lodge till we came to the falls about two miles to the westward of Triconderoga where we encamped, about ten oclock. We with difficult provided covering for the sick, but myself with the well men lay down on the cold ground and nothing but the Heavens to cover us.

11. Eirly in the morning went over to the landing at Lake George. one mile-and a half, to procure a team to carry the sick with some baggage, which I soon did. and likewise got boats so that as soon as the sick came up we wer almost ready to go which we did about twelve o'clock. By this time it rained considerably but we could get no shelter where we was so that we concluded to go notwithstanding, but it rained most of the after noon. We rowed about ten miles, in about two [miles] of Sabath-day point so caled where we encamped. At night the rain increasing which made it very distressing for the sick especially.

12 Friday. Awoke in the morning all over wet but we soon got aboard & went on our way, but the wind being greatly against us we put in at Sabathday point and taried till after eleven oclock. We put out & proceeded on our way but the wind continuing against us we got but about five or six miles to a bunch of small islelands, on one which we landed in order for

lodging. What will become of us I know not for we have nothing to eat but flour nor to drink but lake water nor smoke but oak leaves.

13. In the morning we proceeded on our way & arived at Fort George in the after noon. With difficulty found an empty barrack where we put the sick and delivered them to the Hospital surgeon, then drink some refreshment, eat supper, pitched our tent and lay down for sleep. Ordered to set out for Crown point tomorrow morning.

14 Sunday. The wind shifting last night and this morning it blew hard in the north and continued all day so that we was obliged to tarry all day tho not contrary to our inclinations, it being much better living here than any place we have been at of late.

15. All the morning in preparation for going to Crown Point and about twelve OClock at noon we sat out & roaed to an isleland twelve miles from the point. We landed, pitched our tents, lay down for sleep.

16 Tuesday. Very early in the morning the wind blew strong in the south. We went aboard & hoisted sail and went at a fine rate and arived at the landing a little after nine. Walked to Ticonderoga where we encamped for the night. Accidentally — ——— ——— Ely ——— last who came up by commission from the Governor to the army confirmed the account of the French fleet haveing arived at Rode Isleland.

17 Wednesday. Learned that the Regiment was comeing down to this place this day. Waited all for them till about sun set when they arived. Heard of the death of Colo. Williams which hapned about a week ago at Skeensborough.

18. Taried in camp all day. Nothing material hapning this day till towards night it began to rain, a prospect of a very uncomfortable night.

19. Last night it rained excessive hard. Drove in upon us so that it wet us much. In the morning our cloths were all

wet. Have not had but one so uncomfortable night since I been in the camp.

20. In the morning the Regiment was ordered over on the opisite side for to clear a place for an encampment which they did. Myself went with them all day.

21 Sunday. Went over again on the point & Dr Watson with myself began to build a shelter of logs &c to cover us. Labourd myself most of the day.

22. In the morning returned to labour at my house again. At night got it almost finished except the covering. Returned greatly woried, ate my supper & lay down for sleep. By all that appears it seems we are to make a stand here and as soon as the encampments are fixed they will go to fortifying which the General is in great hurry for.

23 Tuesday. Unwell all day. Taried in the tent. Went not to our new encampment this day.

24. Taried in the forenoon intending to go over in the after noon but it rained so that we went not over this day.

25. Removed bagg & baggage across the Lake but Dr Watson & myself both unwell so that we did nothing to our house, but at night went into a tent and lay down for sleep.

26 Friday. Talk of removing the encampment which if we are Orderd to there will be great uneasiness not only in this Regiment but in most of the Brigade.

27 Saturday. This day Col Porter informs us that General Gates read him a letter from a Gentleman of veracity, as he said, giving an account for Certainty that a French fleet of fifty sail & 15000 foot may be expected in Canada soon.

28 August Monday. Have been so unwell ever since the 27th that I was not able to take down any minutes of the publick afairs or indeed private. For the most part of the time not able to set up two minutes at a time. The 2d past recievd a very

kind letter from my Father & this day have rote an answer which I expect will go to morrow morning. The report is that the fleet has actually arived at Quebec.

6. This morning Mr. Sikes sat out & carried my letter to my Father. This day feel pretty comfortable but I recover not my strength. The regiments on the ground are constantly employed in fortifying and tis said they have got in forward but I have not been able to see them yet.

7. Much better this day. I recover as fast as can be expected. Blessed be God for it. Numbers deserted last night out of this Regt.-This day Leut Whitcomb returned, who had been out as a spy & brings accounts different from what we have heard of late. He said that at St. Johns the Enemy are 4000 strong & at St Chambly about 1000. He kild one oficer in the scout.

8 Thursday. Nothing material this day.

9. Recover my health as fast as can be expected. Walkd down near the water side this day about half a mile, by much the farthest I have been since I was unwell.

10. Walked down & vieud the brest work. Returned much woried but I believe it will be of service to me. Supt on whooclebuerys [huckelebrries] & milk, the finest supper I ever eat.

11 Sunday. Much better. It being a very rainy day walk not abroad this day.

12. Rainy this day also. Oblidged to keep retird.

13. A little more poorly, perhaps owing to the bad weather of late. Deaths happen very frequently. One died yester day very suddenly, & this day Ezekiel Migholl of Hatfield being by appearance but a little poorly died suddenly, a tricking instance of mortallity.

14. Continue unwell, but upon the whole gain strength. Country living is greatly desire & doubt not but I should

recover soon could I enjoy it but I cannot, therefore content myself with my condition & not let it worry my mind, considering this is the place providence has cast my lot for the present, & God is my keeper who is omnipresent, who will not forsake those that forsake not him, tho in the wilderness.

15. Great uneasiness in the camp on account of devouring beef-heads & if they are not redressed soon I doubt not but that great difficulties will arise, but I cant but think that the General will see the inpolicy of it & set matters right soon.

16. This day Leut John Dickinson of Hatfield came to see me which revived me in my weak & low state, new recruits come in almost every day. Four companys of Col Woodbridges Regiment already arived. Some talk that the Col & Leut Col will be broke on account of their inoculating but I cannot at present see the justice of even any uneasiness about it.

17. Continuing unwell tho upon the whole I gain, & indeed as fast as can reasonable be expected beer considering the disadvantages with respect to diet, which if it were proper would perform the whole cure.

18 Sunday. This day Capt Gray from Westfield arived here with his company & says that Springfield companys east & west was to march in about a week after him.

19. It seems to be the general opinion among the Oficers that the Enemy will be upon us pretty soon but I can hardly fall in with them in opinion. But should such a thing happen I think we are in but a poor situation to defend ourselves tho much the best that ever have been since I came into the army, but near one half of the army are now unfit for duty & the rest by no means well, carying almost the simtoms of death in their countenances. Deaths happen more frequent than ever.

20. —
21. —

22 Thursday. Recover my health considerably, but it is enough to move the heart of a stone to be in the situation of a

Phisician under the present circumstances for the distresed to be constantly. calling upon them & not the least thing in the world to relieve them. But as disagreeable as it [is] this is our case & I now dispair of its being better till our time is out, excepting its not being so sickly as cool weather comes on.

23. This day near night Springfield Company arived at Ticonderoga. Leut Noah Wariner I hear is there but I have not seen any of them but expect he will come over here to morrow. Dr. Watson is gone to Fort George having encouragement of a supply of Medicine, but I fear his expectations will be not of now as they have been ever since we have been forced into a Regiment.

26 Monday. Nothing material hapining since the 23d instant. A very cold storm of rain this day which I fear will be very detrimental to the lives and health of the army. As to myself, have arived (through the goodness of God) to a comfortable state of health tho not to my full strength.

27. Cloudy & cold but not much rain. Numbers both Oficers & Soldiers taken ill. & if there is not something more effectually done than at present I fear in a short space we shall not have well men enough to carry off the sick. A report is propagated that there has been a bloody battle at New York & that the Enemy were repulsed with great loss, but it wants confirmation. The loss on our side is said to be 900, on the Enemy side 9000.

28 Wednesday. Recievd no confirmation of the news from York, therefore concluded there is nothing in it. Weather cloudy & cold yet.

29. Dr. Watson returns from Fort George but has brought no supply of medicine as was expected, haveing brought only a small box which in all probability will be gone in about a week .

30. About sun set I was taken with an ague followed with a fever.

31. Had an uncomfortable night last night. This morning felt better but a dull pain continued all the fore noon. In the after noon felt comfortably but weak.

Sept. 1 Sunday. Comfortable all day till Sun about two hours high. At night an ague came on. I imediately took an Emetick which operated kindly, and caried off the fever allmost entirely Went to bed and slept finely.

2. Awoke in the morning, felt clear & comfortable. in the after noon walked over to Ticonderoga having not been there for the space of a month. Near night returnd without any appearance of disadvantage. Reported for certainty that they are in real action at New York.

3. About two clock PM taken with another ague more severe than I had as yet & followed with a fever equally severe.

4 Wednesday. Rested uncomfortably last night by reason of a large sweat. Felt very weak all day. In the evening unexpectedly seized with a fit tho it proved to be but a small one.

5. This being the day for the ague and accordingly a little after twelve it came on very severe. The ague comonly lasts on me about an hour, the fever upwards of four, but the latter is not so tedious to me as the former tho others complain full as much or more.

6 Friday. This morning recievd kind letters from my two brother, together with some fine presents which made me greatly rejoice. God grant I may have an opportunity to repay such peculiar kindness shown to me in this time of need.

7. Last night there was an alarm. The whole army was ordered to lay upon their arms. This was occationed by a heavy canonade being heard at the northward. Suposed that the Enemy had attact our fleet. Had a very slight turn of the ague last Evening. This morning felt weak. In the after noon the ague came on as usual but neither that nor the fever so severe as common.

11 Tuesday. Nothing material since the 7th. The fever & ague has entirely left me tho very weak. Have concluded to try for a furrow to go home to gether with Capt. Chapin as soon as I can. The news from the northward seems to have come to nothing.

14. Obtained a furlow for three weeks but Capt Chapin & the other Oficers who intend to go home have not but expect to tomorrow morning

15. In the morning Cap. Chapin &c went to General for a furrow but he utterly refused to grant them one.

16. In the morning we endeavored to procure a boat to carry Col Porter (he having got a furlow) & myself to Skeensborough & about half after twelve we set off and arived there about nine.

(End of account of this expedition)

Dr. Merrick again served, this time with the Wilbraham militia, in 1777 for the Bennington Alarm. See Appendix D.

Appendix D – Dr. Samuel F. Merrick's Journal of his service at the Bennington Alarm in 1777

1777. Sept 29. About two in the afternoon set out from home on an expedition to the northern army, arrived at Springfield, tarried till night then dismissed till to morning nine o'clock, passed the river with Leut. King in order to lodge with uncle Merrick. 30 met according to order and after deliberating till about four o clock we proceeded on our march. Leut. King returned to bring up the rear. Went to my uncles to lodge again the company proceeded forward.

Oct. 1. About nine o clock set out, overtook the company at Peas, went in company with them about four miles, put up at Crockers lodged at the next house.
Oct. 2. Seargant Lamb and Brewer with Solomon Warriner & myself proceeded forward in order to put out our horses, went as far as Lanesborough, after much difficulty got entertainment at one Powels near the middle of the town.
3d. Turned to the Eastward Bush Meadow, after much difficulty got our horses put out at East Hoosuch at Major Roger Rose where we lodged.
4th. Took my horse in to Williamstown, sent him back to Sd Rose and marched on foot about four miles on the road to Bennington then turned to the left and went about six miles to one Col Plat.
5th. Sunday marched in about five miles of the way at Tulls mills so called, lodged at one Tyashoke (?)
6th. Set out in the morning and arrived there soon, found that our troops were all ordered up the River, Ordered to encamp till further orders. In the afternoon heard canon briskly towards head quarter; very anxious to hear the event.
7. This day about four O clock canon play very briskly followed with small arms & continued till dark, went upon guard this night.
8. This morning an express arrived from head quarters informing that Gen. Gates had caried sundry Redoubts & all the Enemys out lines and twas expected by the motions that they would retreat soon, likewise with orders for us to Press forward with all dispatch, accordingly half after twelve we marcht and travilled till sunset about twelve miles.

9. Gen. Barly from N. Hampshire lodged in the same house with us last night, two expresses arrived informing that the enemy were actually on the retreat, orders for us to make no delay in order to harass them upon their retreat. Set out very early and arrived at Batter Hill before noon about three miles from Saratoga. A very rainy afternoon. Soon after our arrival there was an alarm that the Enemy was upon us, but it proved to be false.
10. Lodged in a corn house last night, about midnight there was another allarm but this likewise Proved false. In the morning concluded to join Col. Porter, but before we did he marched down to the river, we followed on but was ordered more to the southward, which we obeyed and reconoitering the shore found a boat ashore which we were guarding when a number of others came floating down which we took, lodged here this night.
11. Had a very uncomfortable night having nothing but my great Coat to cover myself, in the morning ordered to come here till further orders, this day tooch sundry other boats.
12. Continue still to guard the boats, the Enemy are now about a mile below the church, there has been a scattering fire ever since the retreat bgan and still continues nothing material happening the army excepting Gen. Gates sent in a flagg demanding surrender, but I have heard no answer. This morning Gen. Nickson made an attack upon the enemy but by mistake Gen. Learned who was to attack them in the west at the same time delayed about fifteen minutes after a severe fire a few minutes was obliged to retreat
13. Nothing material
14. Ordered that there be a cessation of arms till sun set. Sundry flaggs passing back and forth, in the evening reported that Gen. Burgoine had agreed to resign himself and army Prisoners of war, to march out to morrow morning.
15. Went over to Saratoga in expectation of seeing the Enemy march out, and after waiting the whole day was obliged to return without having my expectations answered but with great confidence reported that the stipulation was actually signed and that it was to take place to morrow.
16. Waiting to see the army march out but by some reason or other is delayed, towards evening heard that it was put off till tomorrow.

17. *A day never to be forgotten by the American States.* About Eleven O clock A. M. Gen. Burgoine with a number of Other officers rode out, escorted by sundry officers of the Continental army and a little south of the church was met by Gen. Gates, and after a polite compliment proceeded to head quarters; about two the army began to march out. I taried till after four when I returned. They had not all then marched out, but I believe nearly, the number can by no means ascertain but should be inclined to think between five and six thousand but I am by no means a competent judge, tho' I had a good view of them. The Lord be praised for this wonderful token of divine favor for which we cannot be sufficiently thankfull."

End of Journal

Appendix E - Letter to Dr. Samuel Merrick from Col. Joseph Trumbull of Connecticut

Dear Sir -- I have frequently recollected with great satisfaction, the visit you was so good as to make me at Mrs. Lathrop's, two years ago, and your very interesting account of the retreat of the army from Canada in 1776, and their miserable sufferings by small pox, fatigue, and privation.

May I ask the favor of you to commit to writing your recollections of that period, from the death of General Thomas, or earlier, to the end of the campaign. I am induced to write my reminiscences of that period; and as your account is the most perfect corroboration of mine, I shall be in the highest degree obliged to you to furnish them.

J. T.

(Answer)
June 1, 1836.

Sir -- It is some time since I received your kind letter. Should have answered it sooner, but my health was poor. I am now better.

As to the northern expedition, I find by my minutes then kept, that on the 21st of May, 1776, at Sorel, where the river of that name enters the St. Lawrence, the army was on its retreat from Quebec, commanded by General Thomas, who on that day broke out of the small pox. We soon retreated up the river to Chambly, forty-five miles, and ten from St. John's. General Thomas was carried with us, and on the 2d of June he died. It has been said that he died at Sorel, but it is a mistake -- he died at Chambly. On the 20th of June we marched to St. John's, and about sunset we went on board boats for the Isle aux Noix. Orders were peremptory not to stop a moment. There were but two rowers to a boat; they rowed till I thought they would fall from their seats. I, who was not obliged to go on fatigue duty, could not see the men so worried, took an oar myself, and rowed half the night. We arrived at the Isle aux Noix about two hours before day; the sick were thrown on shore, and in five minutes the boats were on their return. I was left with the sick.

I had tents, but I could not pitch them in the night. I covered the sick up as well as I could, and waited for day. I determined not to lie down myself; I attempted to walk, but could not without running over the sick; stand still I could not, for so great was my fatigue that I was afraid I should fall asleep. I was obliged to lie down on the wet grass, and slept about one hour. As soon as it was light I sprang up, examined my sick -- found them asleep. I left them and walked around the island, and found the sick of the whole army in the same situation, amounting to thousands, some dead, others dying. Great numbers could not stand, calling on us (the physicians) for help, and we had nothing to give them. It broke my heart, and I wept till I had no more power to weep. I wiped my eyes, pitched my tents, and others did the same, so that in about an hour, they (the sick) were all out of sight. On the 18th day the whole army arrived, and the island was full of men: on the 19th, I was ordered with the sick to Crown Point, but did not start till next day at twelve o'clock. We passed over the lake -- nothing happened worth mentioning. On the 25th, we arrived at Crown Point, and on the 2d of July, at night, the whole army arrived. On the 10th, I was ordered forward again, with the sick, to Fort George. We took at much pork and flour as we thought we should want; but the pork was bad, and we were obliged to throw it overboard, so that we had nothing but flour wet with lake water, and baked on flat stones. We expected to be but two days in going, but the wind was against us, and we were four days: it looked as if we should all starve. I thought I could eat a tenpenny nail, but we got in and were supllied; the next day we went back, and soon arrived in camp.

It may be thought by some, that I make more out of the sickness than I need. Who has not read of thousands being sick? -- but that is not like seeing it; perhaps such a sight did not occur during the whole war. I believe that at not time was sickness so prevalent, -- besides, they all arrived at night, on a small island; had it been day they would have pitched their tents, but now they could not. Everybody who has seen an army, knows that reading of ten thousand men and seeing them, makes very different impressions; this was very much so with me. I had often read of ten thousand men drawn up in battle array, but I had an imperfect idea of it until I saw Burgoyne's and Gate's army.

As everything relating to the revolutionary war is important, I will just touch upon the taking of Burgoyne. My northern campaign ended with Ticonderoga, and I returned to private life; but in September following, when Burgoyne was marching triumphant through the country at the head of a victorious army, every face gatherd in paleness. I forgot my rank and enlisted as a volunteer to oppose his progress; I repaired to the scene of action, and arrived within five miles of the first decisive battle. Those who have not been within hearing of a battle, can have no adequate idea of it. Words will not describe it -- I shall not attempt it. After that we were ordered up the river, on the heights opposite to Saratoga; thence I had a fine view of the two armies. Burgoyne passed the creek, Gates encamped at Saratoga. My captain called for volunteers to pass the river to headquarters for ammunition; I appeared the first. We came and were admitted to a log hut, the only building left standing by the enemy -- Gates and his officers were there. The captain made me spokesman; I told the general who we were, and that we wanted ammuntion. "Good boys," says he, "to come and help us -- yes, I have ammunition, but drink some punch first," which we accepted. Whilst we were drinking, he says to his officers, "I have just received a very begging letter from brother Burgoyne; he says he has sent me one of his girls, and wishes I would treat her well. I thought he knew me better than to think I would abuse a woman; no, I love them too well." This alluded to a Major Ackley, if I have the name right, [Ackland,] of the British army, who was wounded and taken prisoner, and Burgoyne sent his wife to him, with a flag and this letter; it has lately been published. He then turned to his chief engineer, and says, "they tell me Burgoyne has burned the bridge over the creek; if it is true, how long will it take you to repair it?" "I cannot say; I do not know what materials are at hand."

(Nothing of consequence follows.)

Samuel F. Meyrick (Merrick)
Wilbraham

Appendix F – Revolutionary Soldiers for the Town of Wilbraham

Town	Name / DOB	Rank / DOD	Age	Cemetery
-	**Abbott, Joseph**	Sgt		
	-	3/2/1777	-	-

Signed Non-consumption Pledge in 1774. Enlisted for Capt. Cadwell's Co. on 12/25/76. Sent to Ft. George with smallpox 2/15/77 and died there. Served 2 months, 8 days at Ticonderoga.

Town	Name / DOB	Rank / DOD	Age	Cemetery
Wilb.	**Abbott, Reuben**			
	1761	Jan 28, 1782	21	Adams

In Capt. Phineas Stebbins' Co., Col. Nathan Sparhawk's Regt. Enlisted 9/15/78, discharged 11/17/78. Also 6 months service, enlisted 7/3/1780 in Capt. Abel Holden's Co., Col. Thomas Nixon's Regt. Discharged 12/13/80. Age 19, 5'7", Light complexion.

Town	Name / DOB	Rank / DOD	Age	Cemetery
-	**Adams, Enos**	Sgt		
	1755	-	-	-

Under Capt. John Carpenter 3/21/79 - 6/21/79, 7/6/79 - 10/6/79, and 1/11/80 - 5/5/80. Probably from Brookfield, MA.

Town	Name / DOB	Rank / DOD	Age	Cemetery
-	**Adams, John**			
	-	3/24/1828	95	Adams

From S.A.R. records

Town	Name / DOB	Rank / DOD	Age	Cemetery
Hamp.	**Ainsworth, Luther**			
	-	10/19/1780	-	-

Capt. John Carpenter's Guards at Springfield 10/19/79 - 4/20/80. Capt. Levi Ely's Co., Col. John Brown's Regt, enlisted 7/20/1780 for 3 months. Died in battle along with 45 others near Little Falls (west of Albany) when Brown's Regiment, marching up the Mohawk River to relieve the New York frontier was ambushed by a party of Indians and Tories who were defeated later that same day at Fox's Mills by General Van Rensselear. John Wilson Chaffee also died in same battle.

Town	Name / DOB	Rank / DOD	Age	Cemetery
-	**Ainsworth, Nathan**	Ensign		

Signed Non-consumption Pledge in 1774. Son of "Ensign Nathan" who is buried at Adams

Wilb. **Albert, Moses**
Also Alrert. Residence also given as Granby. Enlisted for 9 months on 6/16/78 at Fishkill, NY, but did not pass muster, having lost half of one foot.

Wilb. **Allen, David**
Also Allin. Age 25, 5'10" ruddy complexion. 6 months service 7/3/80 - 12/17/80, deserted.

Wilb. **Allen, Emmons**
6 months for Wilbraham, 7/3/80 - 1/3/81

\- **Alvord, Aaron** Sgt
Also Alvard. Pvt. in Nov 1754. Signed Non-consumption Pledge in 1774. Marched on the Lexington Alarm of 4/20/75. Served 10 days.

\- **Amidon, John**
1765 4/22/1843 78 Hampden
Also Amadon. 3 months with Capt. Carpenter 1/28/81 - 4/1/81. Born in Ellington, CT.

Hamp. **Amidon, Titus**
Also Amadon. 6 months service 7/6/80 - 12/16/80. Age 17, 5'7", dark complexion. Capt. Abel King's Co., Col. Sears Regt 8/20/81 - 11/20/81 at Saratoga. Lived around 86 Glendale Rd, Hampden. Wife and children buried at the Old Yard in Hampden.

Spgfld **Ashley, Stephen**
4/28/1745 3/21/1820 74 Longmeadow
To Ticonderoga w/Capt. Daniel Cadwell. Enlisted 12/25/76, muster 2/24/77, Discharged 4/2/77 (99 days)

Wilb. **Atchinson, Benoni** Cpl
Signed Non-consumption Pledge in 1774. With Capt. Langdon 4/20/75 - 5/2/75. Possibly 3 months in 1777 as well. Lived at 720 Stony Hill Rd. Family owned 687 Stony Hill as well.

Wilb. **Badger, Joseph**
2/28/1757 5/5/1846 - (d. Ohio)
Capt. Nathan Watkins' Co., Col. John Patterson's Regt in 1775 (DAR). Moved to Perrysburg, Ohio in 1800 as a Minister and died there. Served as Chaplain in the War of 1812.

Spgfld **Bannister, Benoni**
Also Banister. To Ticonderoga w/Capt. Daniel Cadwell. Enlisted 12/25/76, muster 2/24/77, Discharged 4/2/77 (99 days). With Capt. John Carpenter's Guards 5/1780 - 2/17/81 at Springfield (9/17/80 - 2/17/81 at North River, NY).

Wilb. **Bannister, Levi** Fifer
Residence possibly Springfield. Marched 4/20/75 with Capt. Paul Langdon, discharged 5/1/75. Fifer in Capt. Henry's Co., Col. Brewer's Regt 6/4/75 thru at least 8/1/75. Enlisted 12/26/1776 and served as a drummer 1/1/77 - 3/1/1779 in Capt. Charles Colton's Co., Col. Greaton's Regt, then deserted. Returned July 20, 1780 as Pvt. thru end of 1780. 5'3" tall, light complexion, brown hair, light eyes, age 25.

Wilb. **Banton, Jonas**
Capt. Charles Colton's Co, Col. Greaton's Regt 1/1/77 - 1/23/78. Deserted but returned and served through 11/1/78. Enlisted 11/14/1776. 5'8" tall, Light Complexion. Light Hair, Dark eyes. 29 years old. Paid 4,10,0. Children buried at the Old Yard in Hampden.

\- **Barber, Moses**
To Ticonderoga w/Capt. Daniel Cadwell. Enlisted 12/25/76, muster 2/24/77, Discharged 4/2/77 (99 days). In Capt. Ephraim Chapin's Co., Col. Woodbridge's Regt. 8/28/77 - 11/29/77 for Northern Army.

Methuen? **Barker, Nathan**
1761 10/8/1849 88 East Wilb
Deacon. "A soldier of the Revolution" on stone. Enlisted 3/17/81 for 3 years in Capt. John Williams' Co., Col. Joseph Vose's Regt. Born in Pomfret, CT.

Wilb. **Bates, Simeon**
With Capt. Paul Langdon in Col. Timothy Danielson's Regt. at Roxbury. Shows on muster roll of 10/6.

Ludlow **Beckwith, Ichabod**
Marched on 4/20/75 with Capt. Paul Langdon in Col. Timothy Danielson's Regt. to Roxbury. Enlisted in to the army 4/29/75. Shows on muster rolls of 8/1. Named in letters in Nov. 75 from Capt. Langdon for "Bounty Coat".

Wilb. **Beebe, David**
Enlisted 6/30/1781 for 3 years in Capt. Luke Hitchcock's Co., Col. Jos. Vose's 1st Regt. Age 17, 6', light complexion, light hair, farmer.

- **Beebe, Ebeneezer**
1841 11/2/1782 41 Hampden
Signed Non-consumption Pledge in 1774. To Ticonderoga w/Capt. Daniel Cadwell. Enlisted 12/25/76, muster 2/24/77, Discharged 4/2/77 (99 days)

Wilb. **Beebe, Eli**
Wilb Baptist Church. Marched on 4/20/75 With Capt. Paul Langdon in Col. Timothy Danielson's Regt. at Roxbury, but did not march on 4/20. Enlisted in the army 5/4/75. Shows on muster roll of 8/1. Named in letters in Dec. 75 from Capt. Langdon for "Bounty Coat".

Ludlow **Beebe, Ezekiel**
Marched on 4/20/75 with Capt. Paul Langdon in Col. Timothy Danielson's Regt. to Roxbury. Enlisted in the army 4/29/75. Shows on muster rolls of 8/1 and 10/6. Named in letters in Dec. 75/Jan. 76 from Capt. Langdon for "Bounty Coat". Also, Enlisted for Ludlow on 5/12/77 for 3 years in Capt. Oliver's Co., Col. Greaton's Regt., discharged 12/31/79. Part of this time as a drummer.

Hamp. **Beebe, Jonah** Ensign
- 3/26/1831 80 Hampden
Owned 421 Glendale Rd, Hampden, before 1795. Built school at 320 Glendale in 1796.

Hamp. **Beebe, Samuel** Lt
- 10/1/1786 61 Adams
Moved from East Haddam, CT. about 1772 with his son Steward. Signed Non-consumption Pledge in 1774. Lived at 116 Mountain Rd, Hampden, at one time.

Hamp. **Beebe, Steward** Captain
1752 6/13/1823 72 Hampden
Some records have first name as Stewart. Private in Daniel Cadwell's Co 12/25/76 - 4/2/77. In Capt. Ephraim Chapin's Co., Col. Ruggles Woodbridge's Regt 8/15/77 - 10/20/77. Captain of South Co (12th) in 1790. Received his commission from John Hancock. Came from East Haddam,

CT, with his father Samuel in 1772 to 85 North Rd. In 1796 owned 41 Mountain Rd, Hampden.

- **Beebe, Zadock**
Also sp. Zadoc. To Ticonderoga w/Capt. Daniel Cadwell. Enlisted 12/25/76, muster 2/24/77, Discharged 4/2/77 (99 days)

- **Bemont, Sebe**
To Ticonderoga w/Capt. Daniel Cadwell. Enlisted 12/25/76, muster 2/24/77, Discharged 4/2/77 (99 days)

Wilb. **Benton, Zadoc**
Signed Non-consumption Pledge in 1774. Enlisted 6/29/78 for 9 months at Fishkill, NY in Capt. Stebbins's Co., Col. Bliss's Regt. Age 17, 5'1", Brown hair. At Fort Arnold 7/10/1778.

Wilb. **Bird, Reuben**
Enlisted for 9 months under resolve of 6/8/79. Age 17, 5'5" dark complexion, brown hair. In Capt. Abel King's Co., Col. John Bliss's Regt. Starting 7/19/79.

Palmer **Bishop, Eleazer** Pvt
- 3/29/1846 82 Glendale
In Capt. David Speer's Co., Col. Pynchon's Regt. Marched on Lexington Alarm. Served 9 days.

- **Bishop, Samuel** Lt
- - - - Glendale?
Found Wife's gravestone only. No record of being a Lt. In Rev. War.

Palmer **Blackmore, Thomas**
To Ticonderoga w/Capt. Daniel Cadwell. Enlisted 12/25/76, muster 2/24/77, Discharged 4/2/77 (99 days).

- **Bliss, Aaron** Cpl
5/9/1761? 1776 - -
Part of military expedition to Hatfield in August 1748 for 58 days under Capt. Isaac Colton. Signed Non-consumption Pledge in 1774. Died in 1776 as part of Army of Canada.

Wilb. **Bliss, Abel, Jr.**
10/5/1738 11/23/1821 82 Adams
Town Clerk 1811-12. In Church records, 1760. Birthdate 10/16? Son of Ensign Abel Bliss. Justice of the Peace 1814.

Home at 288 Main St. Wilb. Signed Non-consumption Pledge in 1774. No State records for Rev.

- **Bliss, Daniel** Sgt
Signed Non-consumption Pledge in 1774. No State records as Sgt. Possibly in Capt. Gideon Burt's Co. 3/2/77 - 4/10/77 at Ticonderoga.

Wilb. **Bliss, David** Sgt
4/9/1745 10/5/1828 84 Adams
With Capt. Paul Langdon at Roxbury 4/20/74 - 5/15/75. Capt. Reuben Munn's (Monson) Co., Col. Nicholas Dike's Regt at least 9/76 - 11/76. With Capt. James Shaw at Bennington 9/24/77 - 10/18/77. In Capt. John Carpenter's Co. of Guards at Springfield 3/11/79 - 6/11/79 and 6/25/79 - 9/25/79. Possibly more service.

Spgfld **Bliss, Isaac** Pvt
To Ticonderoga w/Capt. Daniel Cadwell. Enlisted 12/25/76, muster 2/24/77, Discharged 4/2/77 (99 days). Enlisted for 3 months in Cont. Army. 7/16/80 - 10/10/80. Age 20, 5'7", ruddy complexion, dark hair, dark eyes, farmer.

Hamp. **Bliss, John, 2d** COL
1727 11/3/1809 83 Hampden
Selectman, State Rep. Senator. Judge. Delegate to 3 provincial congresses. Signed Non-consumption Pledge in 1774. Captain in new Co. formed 7/29/1774. Marched with Capt. Paul Langdon to Roxbury - served 4 days (4/20 - 4/23). Promoted to Major in Aug. 1774. Commissioned Lt. Col. 2/8/76 to replace Col. Pynchon, who resigned. Regimental commander 1st Regt, BG Timothy Danielson's Brigade on 7/5/79. Colonel 10/3/1777 to 1781. Resigned commission due to failing health. Moved from Longmeadow in 1750 to 128 Somers Rd, Hampden. In 1763 owned 142 South Rd.

- **Bliss, Luther**
To Ticonderoga w/Capt. Daniel Cadwell. Enlisted 12/25/76, Discharged 4/2/77 (99 days)

Wilb. **Bliss, Oliver** 2LT
11/20/1736 4/6/1805 69 Adams
Son of Ensign Abel Bliss. Signed Non-consumption Pledge in 1774. Marched 4/20/75 to Roxbury with Capt. Langdon,

discharged 5/5/75 (15 days). In Capt. Charles Colton's Co., Col. John Greaton's Regt on 3/29/79. Enlisted 3/1/1777 for 3 years, discharged 12/31/79. 5'4" tall, Dark Complexion. Dark Hair, Light eyes. 16 years old. Paid 4,10,0. Capt. Joseph Williams' Co., Col Greaton's 3rd Regt 9/79 - 11/79. Enlisted for 3 months 1/1/80 - 3/1/80 with Capt. Colton.

Wilb. **Bliss, Stephen**
1740 2/14/1806 74 -
Signed Non-consumption Pledge in 1774. Enlisted 9/15/78 for 3 months in Capt. Phineas Stebbin's Co., Col. Nathan Sparhawk's Regt. Also 3 months, 7-24-80 - 10/10/80 in Capt. Joseph Browning's Co., Col. Seth Murray's Regt.

Wilb. **Bliss, Thomas** Cpl
11/25/1747 11/28/1830 83 Adams
Signed Non-consumption Pledge in 1774. Marched with Capt. John Langdon to Roxbury - served 12 days (4/20 - 5/2). Enlisted in Capt. Ephraim Chapin's Co, Col. Ruggles' Regt 8/15/77 - 11/30/77 for Northern Army under Gen. Gates (Bennington). Also, Private in Capt. Jos. Hoar's Co., Col. Gideon Burt's Regt. In 6/16/1782 in support of government (Shay's: Samuel Ely incident).

Wilb. **Bond, Israel**
12/1760 - - -
Capt. Job Whipple's Co., Col Rufus Putnam's Regt. 1/27/79 - 12/31/79, Corporal 1/1/80 - 12/31/80. Thropugh 4/81 at West Point. Enlisted 1/27/79, age 20, 5'10 1/2" dark complexion, dark hair, blue eyes.

Wilb. **Boston, Bacchus**
A black soldier from Wilbraham, he enlist enlisted for Springfield on 3/12/81. Age 30, 5'6", black complexion, black hair, laborer/farmer. In Capt. Watson's Co., 3rd Regt. for 3 years. In Capt. James Tisdale's Co., Col. Michael Jackson's Rgt. in 1783, reported deserted in Philadelphia on 8/17/83.

Hamp. **Bradley, Jeremiah**
- 12/20/77 - -
Capt. Charles Colton's Co., Col. John Greaton's 2nd Regt. Enlisted 1/21/1777. 5'10" tall, Light Complexion. Light Hair, Light eyes. 26 years old. Died 12/20/77.

Wilb. **Brewer, Charles** Pvt
12/18/1745 12/23/1836 88 -
First person baptized in Wilbraham Meeting House. Marched on the Lexington Alarm of 4/20/75. Served 2 days. Also See 3rd Regt Muster Roll.

Wilb. **Brewer, Gaius** Sgt
8/28/1753 12/5/1825 70 Adams
Home at 719 Stony Hill Rd. Stebbins history and D.A.R says died 12/7/1843. Same man? With Capt. James Shaw at Bennington 9/24/77 - 10/18/77.

\- **Brown, William**
To Ticonderoga w/Capt. Daniel Cadwell. Enlisted 12/25/76, discharged 2/13/77 (51 days)

Monson **Bullard, Josiah**
Marched on 4/20/75 with Capt. Paul Langdon in Col. Timothy Danielson's Regt. to Roxbury. Did not enlist. Discharged 5/2/75. Served 12 days.

Hamp. **Bumpstead, Joseph** Drummer
\- 3/10/1835 89 Hampden
Also sp. Bumstead and Bump. Signed Non-consumption Pledge in 1774. Capt. Reuben Munn's (Monson) Co. at Roxbury 9/17/76 - 12/26/76. Enlisted for 6 months 7/18/80 - 12/6/80 at West Point. Age 35, 5'8", light complexion. Lived near Bumpstead & Howlett Hill, Hampden.

Wilb. **Burdick, Adam**
Enlisted for 3 months under resolve of 6/2/80. Age 23. In Capt. Joseph Browning's Co., Col. Seth Murray's Regt. 7/24/80 - 10/10/80.

Wilb. **Burdick, Peleg** Pvt
Capt. Reuben Munn's (Monson) Co. at Roxbury 9/17/76 - 11/26/76. Capt. William Sizer's Co., Col. Jeduthan Baldwin's Regt. Enlisted for 3 years. 3/13/1778 - 9/30/1779 then deserted.

Monson **Burr, Timothy** Cpl
At Roxbury with Capt. Langdon. Did not march on 4/20/75. Enlisted 6/8/1775. Listed on Return of 8/1/1775 and Bounty Coat letter of 12/25/75.

Hamp. **Burt, Gideon**
8/16/1745 - - -
Signed Non-consumption Pledge in 1774. Marched on the Lexington Alarm of 4/20/75. Served 2 days. In 1793, lived at 41 Mountain Rd in Hampden

Wilb. **Burt, Moses** Sgt
- 7/15/1787 - Adams
Signed Non-consumption Pledge in 1774. Marched from Chelmsford to Ticonderoga, discharged at Albany on 1/1/77, unsure what unit. Enlisted in Capt. Moses Harvey's Co., Col. David Wells' Regt. 5/10/77 – 7/10/77.

Spgfld **Burt, Oliver**
To Ticonderoga w/Capt. Daniel Cadwell. Enlisted 12/25/76, muster 2/24/77, Discharged 4/2/77 (99 days)

Wilb. **Butler, Joseph**
- 1776 - -
Wilb Baptist Church. No State records. Local records say he "Died in the Arme."

Wilb. **Cadwell, Aaron**
12/23/1753 10/6/1805 51 -
Son of Capt. Daniel. With Capt. Paul Langdon in Col. Timothy Danielson's Regt. at Roxbury. Enlisted in the army 4/29/75. Shows on muster roll 8/1 & 10/6. Named in letters in Dec. 75 from Capt. Langdon for "Bounty Coat".

Wilb. **Cadwell, Daniel Jr.** Captain
1/15/1733 3/27/77 44 -
Service prior to Revolution - see Colonial Period. Lived on Ridge Rd in Wilbraham. Signed Non-consumption Pledge in 1774. Sergeant in 1774. Marched as First Lieutenant on 4/20/75 with Capt. Paul Langdon in Col. Timothy Danielson's Regt. to Roxbury. Enlisted in to the army 4/24/75. Shows on muster rolls of 5/17, 5/22, and 10/6. Commissioned by Congress as 2LT on 5/27/75. Captain of 7th Co. 1st Hampshire (Col. Pynchon's) Regt on 5/2/76 - comissioned 6/13/76. December 25, 1776, became Captain in Col. Timothy Robinson's detachment of Hampshire County militia at Ticonderoga. Named in 6/2/77 petition by Eunice (wife) for expenses due for removal of Captain and some men to Skeensborough because they caught smallpox at Ticonderoga in January 1777. Apparently died of smallpox.

Wilb. **Cadwell, Ebeneezer** Lt
3/3/1737 Btwn 1810-20
Brother of Daniel. Marched on the Lexington Alarm of 4/20/75. Served 10 days. 2LT undr Capt. Thomas Stebbins; Jan. 18,1776, commissioned to serve until end of Jan. 1776, name crossed out on role. 4th Gr. Granddaughter in NH has his powder horn with his name made at Fort Edward in 1758. Born in Springfield.

Wilb. **Cadwell, Levi**
10/13/1746 - - -
Signed Non-consumption Pledge in 1774. Marched 4/20/75 with Capt. Paul Langdon, discharged 4/28/75 (8 days).

Wilb. **Cadwell, Stephen**
5/30/1748 - - -
Marched 4/20/75 with Capt. Paul Langdon, discharged 5/3/75 (13 days). Lived on Glendale Rd. in Wilbraham.

New London **Calkins, James**
1750 3/8/1837 - -
Drafted in April 1775 into Capt. Jonathan Calkins' Company in CT and served throughout 1775 and until 9/1/76. He then enlisted in Captain Comstock's Co., Col. Saltonstall's Regt. Saw General Washington near Ft. Independence. Took sick at White Plains, discharged in Nov. 1776. Moved to Wilbraham in 1779. Received pension from Hampden County, MA in 1834.

Wilb. **Calkins, John**
Also Collins, Colkins. Capt. Stebbins' Co., Col. Bliss's Regt. 9 months from arrival at Fishkill (6/16/78).

Wilb. **Calkins, Samuel**
Also Calking, Colkins, and Collins. To Ticonderoga w/Capt. Daniel Cadwell. Enlisted 12/25/76, muster 2/24/77, Discharged 4/2/77 (99 days). Drafted 6/15/78 for 8 months in Col. Greaton's Regt.

Hamp. **Carpenter, Daniel**
1/1/1747 1811 - Vermont
Lived at 340 Glendale Rd. Hampden. Marched on 4/20/75 with Capt. Paul Langdon in Col. Timothy Danielson's Regt. to Roxbury. Enlisted in the army 4/29/75. Shows on muster rolls of 8/1 and 10/6. Was detached in 1775 for

service at Quebec. Served 7/8/1780 – 10/21/1780 in Capt. Nehemiah Houghton's Co. Moved to Monson after the war.

Hamp. **Carpenter, Jesse** Pvt
1749 1843 94 Nelson, NY
Wilb Baptist Church member. Spelled Carpinder in State records. Marched on the Lexington Alarm of 4/20/75. Served 10 days. Enlisted in July 1775 in Capt. Daniel Lyons' Co., Col. Charles Ellsworth's Regt., discharged 12/14/1775. Service for Melrose at various times between April '75 and April '78. Enlisted 9/24/1776 in Capt. Josiah Russel's Co. for 45 days. To Ticonderoga w/Capt. Daniel Cadwell. Enlisted 12/25/76, muster 2/24/77, Discharged 4/2/77 (99 days). Served in Col. Ashley's Regiment at Ticonderoga from 5/7/1777 – 6/23/1777.

Hamp. **Carpenter, John** Captain
- 9/24/1818 76 Glendale
Lived at 585 Glendale Rd. in Hampden. Sgt in Capt. James Sherman's Co. Col. Pynchon's Regt, marched on 4/20/75, served 7 days for Brimfield. Enlisted 4/24/75 and is a Lieutenant in Capt. Joseph Thompson's Co., Col. Danielson's Regt in Roxbury from 5/75 - 12/75. 1st Lt. in 3rd Continental Infrantry 1/76 - 12/76. Captain in Mass. Militia 1777 - 1779. In Capt Joseph Sibley's Co., Col. Danforth Keyes' Regt on 1/4/78 at Rhode Island. Captain in Col. Ezra Wood's 3d Worcester County Regt, Mass. Militia, commissioned 5/26/78. Detached for service at Peekskill, NY, 6/23/78 through 2/2/79 to guard posts and navigation on the Hudson River. Capt. of a company of Guards in Springfield 3/5/79 - 9/81. Captain of company of rejected recruits on fort duty 10/81 - 3/31/83. Built school at 320 Glendale with Jonah Beebe in 1796.

\- **Carpenter, Jotham**
11/28/1750
Possibly originally from Rhode Island. In Col. Israel Chapin's Regiment, enlisted 10/18/1779 for 41 days. In Capt. John Carpenter's Company of Guards at Springfield 3/5/81 - 5/1/81.

Sutton **Carpenter, Reuben**
2/22/1757 10/5/1802 - Sutton, MA
Capt. Abel King's Co., Col. Sears Regt, 8/21/1781 – 3 months at Saratoga. In Capt. John Carpenter's Company of Guards at Springfield 6/24/79 - 9/24/79, 6/1/80 -

9/1/80, and 9/6/80 - 2/6/81. Supposedly also in Capt. Amos Ellis' Co., Col. Seth Bullard's Regt, enlisted 7/27/1780 for 14 days service at Tiverton, RI, but he was already in Capt. Carpenter's Guards at that time (?).

Brimfield **Carpenter, William**
9/24/1721 1809 or 10 - (d. Stafford, CT)
At Lexington in Capt. Anthony Needham's Co. (South Brimfield), Col. Timothy Danielson's Regt, 4/20/75 - 4/27/75. Enlisted 4/29/75 for 8 months with Capt. Joseph Thompson. Continental Army in Col. Mixon's Regt. For Brimfield 4/1/77 – 12/31/79. With Capt. James Browning, Col Seth Murray 7/15/1780 for three months. Born in Wilbraham. Died in Stafford, CT.

Hamp. **Chaffee, Amos**
Son of John Chaffee. In 1769 owned 148 Scantic Rd & grist mill at 307 Scantic Rd, Hampden. Signed Non-consumption Pledge in 1774.To Ticonderoga w/Capt. Daniel Cadwell. Enlisted 12/25/76, Discharged 4/2/77 (99 days)

Hamp. **Chaffee, Asa**
6/5/1734 12/1810 - Hampden
Signed Non-consumption Pledge in 1774. Marched on the Lexington Alarm of 4/20/75. Served 10 days. To Ticonderoga w/Capt. Daniel Cadwell. Enlisted 12/25/76, Discharged 4/2/77 (99 days). Also in 1777, Capt. Aaron Graves' Co., Col. David Leonard's Regt. Born in Woodstock, CT.

Hamp. **Chaffee, Asa, Jr.**
Listed in previous town histories, but no state records.

Hamp. **Chaffee, Comfort, Sr.**
- 6/4/1811 74 Hampden
Lived at 96 South Rd, Hampden Marched on the Lexington Alarm of 4/20/75. Served 10 days. Hampden book says he discovered an abandoned British ship during war and captured it. No specific record of this in State files, but he was at Bristol, RI. In Capt. Hill's Co., Col. John Dagget's Regt at Bristol, RI, Jan-Mar 1776. With Capt. John Pain's Co. at Winter Hill and Dorchester Mar-Apr 1776, and in Capt. (?) Carpenter's Co., Col. Simeon Cary's Regt at White Plains July-Dec 1776. ALso, With Capt. Shaw at Bennington in 1777.

Hamp. **Chaffee, Darius**
3/22/1743-4
Marched on the Lexington Alarm of 4/20/75. Served 3 days. Possibly the same Darius in Capt. William Fletcher's Co 9/5/78 - 10/1/78 at the northward.

Hamp. **Chaffee, Ephraim**
"Scalped by the Indians" according to previous histories, but no record of this in the State files. Served in Capt. Nathan Rowle's Co., Col. John Jacob's Regt. 7/1/78 - 1/1/79 at Rhode Island.

Hamp. **Chaffee, Ephraim, 2nd**
8/12/1760 11/11/1843 84 Hampden
In Capt. Jabez Bullock's Co., Col. Thomas Carpenter's Regt 7/24/80 - 10/10/80 at Tiverton, RI. Age 20.

Hamp. **Chaffee, Isaac**
Lived at 48 Stafford Rd, Hampden, in 1761. In Capt. John Carpenter's Company of Guards at Springfield 1/22/80 - 4/22/80, 4/22/80 - 5/31/80, and 6/8/80 - 8/20/80 (3 month enlistments).

Hamp. **Chaffee, Isaiah, Jr.**
6 months service 7/6/1780 - 12/6/80, Mass. 12th Regt.. Age 16, 5'5", Light complexion. Also, bounty paid 3/8/81 by Lt. Wm. King for 3 years in Cont. Army. Captain Carpenter's Guards 1/24/81 - 40/10/81

Hamp. **Chaffee, John Wilson**
\- 10/19/1780 - -
Lived at 111 Stafford Rd, Hampden, in 1764. Also at 148 Scantic. Signed Non-consumption Pledge in 1774. With Capt. Paul Langdon in Col. Timothy Danielson's Regt. at Roxbury, but did not march. Enlisted in to the army 5/8/75. Shows on muster rolls of 8/1 and 10/6. Was detached during 1775 for service at Quebec. Enlisted in Capt. Charles Colton's Co., Col. John Greaton's 2nd Regt on 3/1/1777 through 12/31/79 (3 years). Capt. Levi Ely's Co., Col. John Brown's Regt, enlisted 7/20/1780 for 3 months. Died in battle along with 45 others near Little Falls (west of Albany) when Brown's Regiment, marching up the Mohawk River to relieve the New York frontier was ambushed by a party of Indians and Tories who were defeated later that same day at Fox's Mills by General Van Rensselear. Luther Ainsworth also died in same battle. 5'7" tall, Dark Complexion. Dark Hair, Light eyes. 22 years old. Paid 4,10,0.

Hamp. **Chaffee, Jonathan**
1753(?) 7/24/1818 65 Hampden
In local histories, but no State records.

Hamp. **Chaffee, Joseph, 3rd**
Various Joseph Chaffee's in war records. Can't identify service.

\- **Chaffee, Josh**
"Jos'h" Marched at the Lexington Alarm with Capt. Warriner. 4/20/75.

\- **Chaffee, Josiah**
Enlisted in Cont. army 4/25/81 for 3 years. Age 17, 5'7", light complexion, light hair, Farmer.

Hamp. **Chaffee, Simeon**
1738(?) 9/13/1824 86 Hampden
Lived at 130 Stafford Rd, Hampden, in 1776. Signed Non-consumption Pledge in 1774. No State Records.

Hamp. **Chaffee, William**
One of the guards of Major Andre, a British officer who was executed as a spy. Lived at 148 Stafford Rd, Hampden, in 1774, 307 Scantic in 1778. Possibly a private in Capt. Joseph Franklin's Co., Col. Thomas Carpenter's Regt at Bristol, RI. Co. marched from Rehoboth, 12/8/76, for 16 days service.

\- **Chanwell, Aaron** Cpl
With Capt. James Shaw at Bennington 9/24/77 - 10/18/77.

Hamp. **Chapin, Abner, Jr.** Cpl
5/29/1749 4/1/1814 - -
Wilb Baptist Church. Signed Non-consumption Pledge in 1774. Marched on 4/20/75 with Capt. Paul Langdon in Col. Timothy Danielson's Regt. to Roxbury. Enlisted in to the army 4/29/75. Shows on muster rolls of 8/1 and 10/6. Detached for service at Quebec during 1775. With Capt. James Shaw at Bennington 9/24/77 - 10/18/77. Saw Burgoyne surrender. Lived at 70 Somers Rd, Hampden, at one time before selling to Samuel Chapin.

West Spgfld **Chapin, Asahel**
1748 1809 - (d. Spgfld)
At Lexington in Capt. Enoch Chapin's Co 4/20/75 - 5/1/75 (11 days) for West Springfield. Enlisted in Capt. Joseph Morgan's Co., Col. John Woodley's Regt for West Springfield for service "northward" 9/21/77 - 10/17/77. Born in Wilbraham. Died in Springfield.

- **Chapin, Benoni** Cpl
7/9/1758 - - Chicopee
To Ticonderoga w/Capt. Daniel Cadwell. Enlisted 12/25/76, muster 2/24/77, Discharged 4/2/77 (99 days). Capt. John Morgan's Co. of Guards at Springfield and Brookfield, 1/5/78 - 7/1/78. Capt. Samuel Burt in New London 7/22/79 – 8/25/79. Corporal in Capt. Joseph Browning's Co., Col. Seth Murray's Regt. 7/21/80 - 10/10/80. Listed in Chicopee history as having been from Chicopee and also being buried there. Chicopee history says he died on 12/25/76, but this is wrong.

Wilb. **Chapin, Daniel**
Home at 742 Glendale Rd., Wilb. To Ticonderoga w/Capt. Daniel Cadwell. Enlisted 12/25/76, muster 2/24/77, Discharged 4/2/77 (99 days).

Hamp. **Chapin, Henry** Lt
- - - Chicopee (?)
Church records in 1760 as Lt. Lived at 148 Scantic Rd, Hampden, in 1753. Also 70 Somers Rd before selling to Abner Chapin. To Ticonderoga w/Capt. Daniel Cadwell. Enlisted 12/25/76, muster 2/24/77, Discharged 4/2/77 (99 days). Listed in Chicopee history as having been from Chicopee and also being buried there.

Spgfld **Chapin, Israel** Lt
Marched with Maj. Andrew Colton 4/20/75 for 10 days service. Enlisted into army 4/29/75. 2LT in Capt. Walter Pynchon's 1st Co., 1st Hampshire Regt, Commissioned 6/13/76. Lieutenant in Capt. Enoch Cooper's Co., Col. David Leonard's Regt. 5/16/77 - 7/15/77 at Ticonderoga. With Capt. James Shaw at Bennington 9/24/77 - 10/18/77.

- **Chapin, Judah** Pvt
To Ticonderoga w/Capt. Daniel Cadwell. Enlisted 12/25/76, muster 2/24/77, Discharged 4/2/77 (99 days).

Hamp. **Chapin, Samuel**
1/30/1762 4/14/1837 75 Hampden
Lived at 70 Somers Rd, Hampden, at one time. Served in Capt. Nathan Rowe's Co, Col. John Jacob's Regt 7/1/78 - 1/1/79 at Rhode Island under Gen. John Sullivan.He was not in the battle of 8/291778 but was in the retreat to the mainland and was then at Tiverton, RI. Served 7/79 for one month under Capt. Samuel Burt and Ensign Simeon Chapin in Col. Porter's command at New London. Received a pension from Hampden County in 1831.

Wilb. **Chapin, Zebulon**
- 10/27/1823 82 -
Marched on 4/20/75 with Capt. Paul Langdon in Col. Timothy Danielson's Regt. to Roxbury. Did not enlist. Discharged 5/2/75. 12 days.

Wilb. **Chase, Isaac**
6 months service starting 10/25/80.

Wilb. **Chase, Isaiah**
7 months for Wilbraham in 12th Mass. Regt. Discharged 12/6/80 at West Point.

Wilb. **Chase, Rufus**
Enlisted for 9 mos for Wilb, resolve of 6/9/79. Capt Abel King's Co., Col. John Bliss's Regt. 7/8/79 - 4/28/80. Age 16, 5'4", dark complexion, brown hair.

- **Chatterton, John** Pvt
Also Charterton. To Ticonderoga w/Capt. Daniel Cadwell. Enlisted 12/25/76, muster 2/24/77, Discharged 4/2/77 (99 days). Also with Capt. James Shaw at Bennington 9/24/77 - 10/18/77.

- **Chubb, Benjamin** Pvt
- 1775 - -
Marched on 4/20/75 with Capt. Paul Langdon in Col. Timothy Danielson's Regt. to Roxbury. Enlisted in to the army 4/29/75. Shows on muster rolls of 8/1 and 10/6. Detached to Quebec, where he died. Reported on 10/6/75 Return as deceased.

-	**Clark, Benoni**	Pvt		

To Ticonderoga w/Capt. Daniel Cadwell. Enlisted 12/25/76, muster 2/24/77, Discharged 4/2/77 (99 days). In Capt. Ephraim Chapin's Co., Col. Ruggles Woodbridge's Regt 8/12/77 - 11/30/77 in the Northern Army.

Belchertown — **Clark, Enos** Pvt

Son of William Clark (below). Marched on the Lexington Alarm of 4/20/75. Served 10 days.

- **Clark, Seth**

1723 — 1790 — - — d. Wilb.

Wilb Baptist Church member. Marched with Capt. Langdon on 4/20 to Roxbury, enlisted. Was "on guard" at Cambridge 5/15/75 under Major Loammi Baldwin. Listed in Bounty Coat letter of 12/25/1776. Also in Capt. Wales' Co of Northhampton. Most likely more service as there are several Seth Clark's listed for Hamp. Regts. Born in Northhampton. Born in Northampton - Served in Capt. Wales' Northahmpton militia

Hartford — **Clark, Stephen**

- — - — - — d. Wilb.

Served for Hartford County, CT in CT Militia. Died at daughter Eunice's house in Wilbraham.

Wilb. — **Clark, William**

1734

Also Belchertown. Marched on 4/20/75 with Capt. Paul Langdon in Col. Timothy Danielson's Regt. to Roxbury. Enlisted in to the army 4/29/75. Shows on muster rolls of 8/1 and 10/6. Named in letters in Jan. 76 from Capt. Langdon for "Bounty Coat". In Lt. Aaron Phelps' Co, Col. Elisha Porter's Regt. 7/9/77 - 8/8/77.

- **Coleman, Thomas** Pvt

Also "Colman". Signed Non-consumption Pledge in 1774. Marched on the Lexington Alarm of 4/20/75. Served 10 days.

Longmdw — **Colton, Aaron** Cpl

12/5/1758 — 6/3/1840 — - — -

Brother of William. Later years in Hartford, CT. To Ticonderoga w/Capt. Daniel Cadwell. Enlisted 12/25/76, muster 2/24/77, Discharged 4/2/77 (99 days).

\- **Colton, Benjamin**
Marched on the Lexington Alarm of 4/20/75. Served 10 days.

\- **Colton, Charles**
In Capt. John Carpenter's Guards at Springfield 6/3/80 - 9/3/81, 10/1/81 - 1/1/82. Also 2/8/82 - 3/31/83 at Castle Island with Co. of rejected recruits.

Wilb. **Colton, Daniel**
Wife buried at East Wilbraham. In Capt. Isaac Colton's Co, Col. David Brewer's 9th Regt. At Roxbury. Enlisted for 3 months on 5/10/75. Bounty Coat letter. Sergeant in Capt. Ephraim Chapin's Co., Col. Woodbridge's Regt 8/23/77 - 10/23/77 in the Northern army. Private in Capt. Abel King's Co., Col. Sears' Regt 8/20/81 - 11/20/81 at Saratoga.

\- **Colton, Ebeneezer** Lt
Not listed in State records.

Ludlow **Colton, Edward**
Also listed as Edward Cotton. Marched on 4/20/75 with Capt. Paul Langdon in Col. Timothy Danielson's Regt. to Roxbury. Enlisted in to the army 4/29/75. Shows on muster rolls of 8/1 and 10/6. Named in letters in Jan. 76 from Capt. Langdon for "Bounty Coat". To Ticonderoga w/Capt. Daniel Cadwell. Enlisted 12/25/76, muster 2/24/77, Discharged 4/2/77 (99 days). Enlisted 10/19/79 for 9 months. Age 25, 5'6" Brown complexion. Private in Capt. Abel King's Co., Col. Sears' Regt 8/20/81 - 11/20/81 at Saratoga.

\- **Colton, Eli**
To Ticonderoga w/Capt. Daniel Cadwell. Enlisted 12/25/76, muster 2/24/77, Discharged 4/2/77 (99 days). Also with Capt. Samuel Burt, Col. Elisha Porter's Regt. 7/22/79 - 8/25/79 at New London.

Spgfld **Colton, Frederick**
Marched on 4/20/75 with Capt. Paul Langdon in Col. Timothy Danielson's Regt. to Roxbury. Enlisted in to the army 4/29/75. Shows on muster rolls of 8/1 and 10/6. Named in letters in Dec. 75 from Capt. Langdon for "Bounty Coat". Enlisted for 3 years in Cont. Army for Springfield

(1/1/77 - 11/14/79) in Capt. Charles Colton's Co., Col. John Greaton's 2nd Regt as a wagoner.

Colton, Gideon
In Capt. John Carpenter's Guards at Springfield 3/11/79 - 5/24/79.

Palmer **Colton, Isaac, Jr.** Capt
Considerable service in the pre-revolutionary years - see Colonial Period. Captain in Col. Brewer's Regt at Roxbury on April 24th, 1775, commissioned 6/17/75, through end of 1775.

Colton, John Sgt/Lt
Sgt in Maj. Andrew Colton's Co.. Marched to Roxbury 4/20, 14 days service. To Ticonderoga w/Capt. Daniel Cadwell. Enlisted 12/25/76, muster 2/24/77, Discharged 4/2/77 (99 days). With Capt. James Shaw at Bennington 9/24/77 - 10/18/77. 2LT in Capt. Samuel Burt's Co., Col. Bliss's Hampshire Regt. Commissioned 4/23/78. 2LT in Capt. Carpenter's Guards 3/11/79 - 9/30/79. 1LT in Capt. Joseph Browning's Co., Col. Seth Murrany's Regt. 7/4/80 - 10/12/80 in Suffolk County. Lieutenant serving as a private in 2d Co., Col. Gideon Burt's Co. marched to retake Samuel Ely and put down rioters at Northhampton 6/12/82 - 6/16/82 (Shay's).

Colton, Joseph Cpl
1745 1817 - -
Son of Benjamin. To Ticonderoga w/Capt. Daniel Cadwell. Enlisted 12/25/76, muster 2/24/77, Discharged 4/2/77 (99 days). Possibly same as Joseph who served under Capt. Abel King at Saratoga in 1781

Wilb. **Colton, Moses**
1724 2/24/1777 53 Adams
Signed Non-consumption Pledge in 1774. Marched on the Lexington Alarm of 4/20/75. Served 10 days. Died of smallpox (not in service).

Colton, Nathan
John Carpenter's Guards at Springfield 3/15/79 - 6/15/79

Spgfld **Colton, William, 3d** Fifer
1/6/1754 5/6/1825

Brother of Aaron. Marched to Roxbury 4/20/75 with Major Andrew Colton's Co. Enlisted 4/29/75 in Capt Gideon Burts Co, Col Timothy Danielson's Regt. Marched with Daniel Cadwell, service at Ticonderoga 12/26/76 - 4/2/77

Wilb. **Conant, Israel** Pvt
Drafted 7/16/79 -4/16/80 (9 mos) in Capt. King's Co., Col. Bliss's Regt. Age 38, 5'6" dark complexion, brown hair.

Hamp. **Cone, Zenas**
- 7/4/1818 54 Hampden
Lived at 94 Mountain Rd, Hampden, in 1798. Drafted for 6 months (7/18/80 - 12/16/80) under Capt. Joseph Brown. Age 16, 5'5", light complexion. Mustered at Camp Tenith near West Point, NY.

Ludlow **Cooley, Charles**
At Roxbury with Capt. Langdon. Did not march on 4/20/75. Listed on Return of 10/6/1775 and Bounty Coat letter of 11/27/75.

Cooley, George
With Capt. James Shaw at Bennington 9/24/77 - 10/18/77.

Spgfld **Cooley, Jabin**
Also Jabez. WIth Capt. Gideon Burt at Roxbuy. Enlisted 4/28/75 for 3 months, 11 days. Bounty coat letter 12/22/75. With Capt. James Shaw at Bennington 9/24/77 - 10/18/77.

Wilb. **Cooley, Jonathan**
Marched on the Lexington Alarm of 4/20/75. Served 10 days.

Longmdw **Cooley, Josiah** Cpl
11/30/1749 1824 - -
DAR credits with Lexington Service, but does not say who he was under. With Capt. James Shaw at Bennington 9/24/77 - 10/18/77.

Cooley, Justin
To Ticonderoga w/Capt. Daniel Cadwell. Enlisted 12/25/76, muster 2/24/77, Discharged 4/2/77 (99 days). Capt. Ephraim Chapin's Co, enlisted 8/12/77, discharged 11/30/77 for service in the Northern army.

Ludlow **Cooley, Luther**
Lt. Enoch Chapin's Co., Col. David Leonard's Regt. At Ticonderoga 5/16/77 - 7/15/77. With Capt. Shaw at Bennington 9/24/77 - 10/18/77. In Capt. Samuel Burt's Co., Col. Elisha Porter's Regt. 7/22/79 - 8/25/79 at New London. Drafted for 3 months 7/17/80 - 10/10/80 in Capt. Joseph Browning's Co, Col. Seth Murray's Regt in Suffolk County. Age 19, 5'6", Ruddy complexion, dark hair, blue eyes, Farmer.

Wilb. **Cooley, Solomon**
Also Ludlow. With Capt. Paul Langdon in Col. Timothy Danielson's Regt. at Roxbury. Enlisted 5/3/75. Named in letters in Nov. 75 from Capt. Langdon for "Bounty Coat".

Wilb. **Corneal, John**
Enlisted for Boston, no year given.

Wilb. **Crane, Stephen**
1734 1778 - -
Marched on 4/20/75 with Capt. Paul Langdon in Col. Timothy Danielson's Regt. to Roxbury. Did not enlist. Discharged 4/22/75, 3 days.

Hamp. **Crocker, Rowland**
- 11/7/1815 79 - -
Lived at 449 North Rd, Hampden, in 1774. Signed Non-consumption Pledge in 1774. Marched on the Lexington Alarm of 4/20/75. Served 10 days.

Windor, CT **Cross, Stephen**
4/15/1755 9/16/1838 82 East Wilb.
3rd Connecticut Regiment under Captains Roger Enos of Windosr and Elijah Robinson of Stafford. Moved to Monson, MA after the war and died in Wilbraham.

Palmer **Cummins, Solomon**
Marched on 4/20/75 under Capt. David Speer, Col. Pynchon's Regt., Served 9 days. To Ticonderoga w/Capt. Daniel Cadwell. Enlisted 12/25/76, muster 2/24/77, Discharged 4/2/77 (99 days). Sent to Ft. George with smallpox 2/1/77. Mentioned in letter for expenses due to smallpox by John McElwain.

Wilb. **Cutt, Joseph**

1734 1/15/1782 - Adams

Also Coot. One of three black soldiers from Wilbraham. Capt. Warriner's Co., Col. Bliss's Regt. , drafted for 6 months 7/7/78. Age 40, 5'4", Black complexion. At Fort Arnold 7/10/1778. In Capt. Kin's Co, Col' Bliss's Regt 7/12/79 - 4/12/80. In Capt. Joseph Browning's Co, Col. Seth Murray's Regt. 7/24/80 - 10/10/80.

Hamp. **Davis, John**

- 2/23/1826 75 Hampden

Lived at 48 Stafford Rd, Hampden, in 1761. Marched on 4/20/75 with Capt. Paul Langdon in Col. Timothy Danielson's Regt. to Roxbury. Enlisted in to the army 4/29/75. Shows on muster rolls of 8/1 and 10/6. Named in letters in Dec. 75/Jan. 76 from Capt. Langdon for "Bounty Coat".

Wilb. **Davis, Kittridge**

Marched on 4/20/75 with Capt. Paul Langdon in Col. Timothy Danielson's Regt. to Roxbury. Enlisted in to the army 4/29/75. Shows on muster rolls of 8/1 and 10/6. Named in letters in Dec. 75 from Capt. Langdon for "Bounty Coat". In Capt. Caleb Keep's Co, Col. Israel Chapin's Regt at Claverack 10/18/79 - 11/21/79. Resolve of 6/5/80, drafted for 6 months (7/18/80 - 1/18/81). Age 21, 5'8", light complexion. Served at West Point, NY.

West Spgfld **Day, Joel**

- - - Holyoke?

Possibly Elmwood Cem. Holyoke (D.A.R.)Marched under Capt. Enoch Chapin to Roxbury 4/20/75, served 35 days. In Capt. Joseph Morgan's Co, Col. John Mosley's Regt in Northern Army 10/21/76 - 11/17/76. To Ticonderoga w/Capt. Daniel Cadwell. Enlisted 12/25/76, muster 2/24/77, Discharged 4/2/77 (99 days). In Capt. Carpenter's Co. of Guards at Springfield, 3/11/79 - 6/11/79, 7/3/79 - 10/3/79, 10/7/79 - 1/1/80, 1/7/80 - 4/7/80, 6/8/80 - 12/9/80 (successive three month enlistments).

Hamp. **Day, Samuel**

Son of Captain Samuel Day? Marched on the Lexington Alarm of 4/20/75. Served 10 days.

Hamp. **Dunham, Ephraim** Cpl

One of five brothers. Marched on 4/20/75 with Capt. Paul Langdon in Col. Timothy Danielson's Regt. to Roxbury. Enlisted in to the army 4/29/75. Shows on muster rolls of 8/1 and 10/6. Named in letters in Dec. 75/Jan. 76 from Capt. Langdon for "Bounty Coat". Corporal in Capt. Joseph Thompson's 1st Co. 4th Regt (LTC Thomas Nixon), Return dated 11/9/76 at North Castle.

Hamp. **Dunham, Gamaliel**

One of five brothers. Private in Captain Rueben Munn's Monson Co. at Roxbury on 9/17/76.

Hamp. **Dunham, Isaac**

One of five brothers. Signed Non-consumption Pledge in 1774. Marched on the Lexington Alarm of 4/20/75. Served 10 days.

Hamp. **Dunham, Joseph**

One of five brothers. Wilb Baptist Church. Marched on 4/20/75 with Capt. Paul Langdon in Col. Timothy Danielson's Regt. to Roxbury. Enlisted in to the army 4/29/75. Shows on muster rolls of 8/1 and 10/6. Named in letters in Dec. 75/Jan. 76 from Capt. Langdon for "Bounty Coat".

Hamp. **Dunham, Malam**

\- 1776 - -

One of five brothers. Supposedly died at Roxbury. No State records to confirm.

Wilb. **Dunn, William Harper**

Marched on Lexington Alarm on 4/19/75 in Capt. John Crawford's Co., Col. Jonathan Warner's Regt. Served 9 days.

Wilb. **Eddy, James**

\- 11/8/1779 - East Wilb.

Wilb Baptist Church Deacon. Capt. Rueben Munn's Monson Co., Col. Nicholas Dike's Regt. At least 9/17/76 - 11/26/76. Probably Capt. Ephraim Chapin's Co., Col. Woodbridge's Regt. 8/15/77 - 9/30/77 in the Northern Dept.

Wilb. **Eddy, Joshua**
Marched on the Lexington Alarm of 4/20/75. Served 10 days.

Bridge Water **Edson, Benjamin**
10/13/1759 8/4/1830 72 Glendale
Capt. Josiah Packard's Co., Col. Edward Mitchell's Plymouth Regt. Joined Daniel Shays in 1787 and was a fugitive in Pelham.

Edson, James
To Ticonderoga w/Capt. Daniel Cadwell. Enlisted 12/25/76, muster 2/24/77, Discharged 4/2/77 (99 days)

East Windsor **Elsworth, Moses**
Marched on 4/20/75 with Capt. Paul Langdon in Col. Timothy Danielson's Regt. to Roxbury. Enlisted in the army 6/30/75. Bounty coat letter 12/25/75. To Ticonderoga w/Capt. Daniel Cadwell. Enlisted 12/25/76, muster 2/24/77, Discharged 4/2/77 (99 days)

Elwell, Jesse
Enlisted for 3 months under resolve of 6/22/80. In Capt. Joseph Browning's Co., Col. Seth Murray's Regt. 7/24/80 - 10/10/80. In Capt. Abel King's Co., Col. Sears' Regt at Saratoga 8/20/81 - 11/20/81.

Wilb. **Ely, Judah**
6/24/1753 5/19/1814 61 Adams
Marched on 4/20/75 with Capt. Paul Langdon in Col. Timothy Danielson's Regt. to Roxbury but did not enlist. Discharged 5/15/75 (25 days). With Capt. James Shaw at Bennington 9/24/77 - 10/18/77.

Wilb. **Farnham, Benjamin**
Marched on the Lexington Alarm of 4/20/75. Served 10 days.

Wilb. **Ferry, Charles** 2LT
Also Ferre & Fare. Marched on 4/20/75 as a drummer with Capt. Paul Langdon in Col. Timothy Danielson's Regt. to Roxbury. Enlisted in the army 4/29/75. Shows on muster rolls of 8/6 & 10/1 and Bounty Coat letter of 11/27/1775. In Capt. Collins Co., Col. Woodbridge's Regt at Ticonderoga 8/25/76 where he was appointed Drum Major. With Capt. James Shaw at Bennington 9/24/77 - 10/18/77. 2LT in

Capt. Caleb Keep's Co., Col. Israel Chapen's Regt, 10/15/79 - 11/21/79 at Claverack, NY. Capt. John Carpenter's Guards 6/20/81 – 9/20/81.

Fisher, Eleazer
To Ticonderoga w/Capt. Daniel Cadwell. Enlisted 12/25/76, muster 2/24/77, Discharged 4/2/77 (99 days)

Wilb. **Fuller, Lothrop**
- - - Ludlow
Also Ludlow. Marched on 4/20/75 with Capt. Paul Langdon in Col. Timothy Danielson's Regt. to Roxbury. Enlisted in to the army 4/29/75. Shows on muster rolls of 8/1 and 10/6. Named in letters in Dec. 75 from Capt. Langdon for "Bounty Coat". Buried at Church Street Cemetery in Ludlow.

Fuller, William
To Ticonderoga w/Capt. Daniel Cadwell. Enlisted 12/25/76, muster 2/24/77, Discharged 4/2/77 (99 days)

Hardwick **Glayser, Benjamin**
Enlisted for Wilbraham, no date given. Age 22, 5'11" dark complexion, dark hair. Deserted Feb. 79.

Wilb. **Glover, John** Lt
1754 7/1789 - Adams
Probably spread Lexington alarm through town in 1775. Lt at Dorchester 1776, Cavalry officer in Continental Army later. Drafted for Capt. Cadwell's Co at one point. Enlisted in Cont. army for Boston at one time. While these last two occurrences were for John of Wilbraham, it seems as though they are at odds with "Lt. John." Possibly two John Glover's?

Wilb. **Goodwill, John**
Enlisted for 3 months under resolve of 6/22/80. Age 16. In Capt. Joseph Browning's Co., Col. Seth Murray's Regt. 7/24/80 - 10/10/80.

Wilb. **Grover, Isaiah**
Also as Isatah and residence as Windsor, CT. Bounty paid 4/4/81 by Thomas Merrick for a class of Wilbraham for 3 years. Age 23 5'9" light complexion, light hair, farmer. In Capt. Hastings' Co., LTC John Brooks Regt. On 4/5/81.

Enfield **Hale, Samuel**
1753 1831 - d. Wilb.
Lexington Alarm under Capt. Simons and service as a corporal under Capt. Hezekiah Parson' Co., Col. Comfort Sage's Regt. All service for Connecticut.

Hamlin, John
1761 1825 - -
Capt. Elijah Blackman's Co., Col. Sherborne's Regt in 1777. Pension in 1818 from Wilbraham. Born in Somers, CT.

Wellfleet **Hamlin, Perez**
- - - Hampden
In D.A.R. records. Service for Wellfleet in Capt. Winslow Lewis's Co. at Cambridge on January 13, 1776.

Hancock, Elijah
- 1779 - -
At Roxbury on 10/7/75 in Capt. Isaac Colton's Co, Col. David Brewer's Regt. Drafted at some point in early 1779 for Hampshire County. Named in findings of a dispute between Springfield and Wilbraham as to which town service was to be credited for. Wilbraham was given credit by the committee (4/16/79). Served in Capt. Chalres Colton's Co., Col. John Greaton's 2nd Regt., reported as deceased.

Hancock, Jabez
To Ticonderoga w/Capt. Daniel Cadwell. Enlisted 12/25/76, muster 2/24/77, Discharged 4/2/77 (99 days)

Hancock, John
Also Hencock. To Ticonderoga w/Capt. Daniel Cadwell. Enlisted 12/25/76, muster 2/24/77, Discharged 4/2/77 (99 days)

Spgfld. **Hancock, Moses**
1759 9/22/1828 68 Glendale
Enlisted for 3 years in 1777 in Capt. Charles Colton's Co., Col. Greaton's Regt. Received a Pension from Wilbraham in 1818. Born in Springfield.

Wilb. **Hendrick, Abijah**
1761 1840 - (d. Feeding Hills)
Capt. John Morgan's Co., 1/9/78 - 7/1/78 to guard stores at Springfield and Brookfield. Born in Wilbraham. Received Hamp. County Pension.

Hill, Asa
In Capt. Joseph Browning's Company, Col. Murray's Regiment

Hill, Jeptha
With Capt. James Shaw at Bennington 9/24/77 - 10/18/77. Enlisted for Wilbraham (in a class) on 5/1/1781 for 3 years. Age 18, 5'3", light complexion, light hair, Farmer.

Hill, Tower
Listed in Steuben's Report of unfit soldiers as enlisting, in a class, but "Decrepit" ("lame in both legs"). 7/12/1781 for bounty by Silas Bliss for three years. Age 22, 5'9", Black complexion, Black Hair, farmer. 3rd Mass. Regt.

Hamp. **Hitchcock, Aaron**
9/1/1756 11/29/1836 80 -
Capt. Rueben Munn's Co., Col. Nicholas Dike's Regt at Roxbury 9/17/76 and 11/26/76 returns. Son of Lt. John.

Hamp. **Hitchcock, John, 3rd** Lt
4/21/1722 10/11/1807 85 (d. Wilb.)
Served on Western Frontier of Mass. 9/2-9/12/1754 under Capt. Isaac Colton. Lived at 300 Wilbraham Rd in 1742 with father Luke. Signed Non-consumption Pledge in 1774. Marched on the Lexington Alarm of 4/20/75. Served 10 days. To Ticonderoga as a private w/Capt. Daniel Cadwell. Enlisted 12/25/76, muster 2/24/77, Discharged 4/2/77 (99 days). In 1778 appointed to look after families of men gone off to war. D.A.R. records say he was also at Bennington but neither state nor town records support this. Born in Springfield, died in Wilbraham.

Hitchcock, Luther
6/13/1754 -
With Capt. James Shaw at Bennington 9/24/77 - 10/18/77.

Wilb. **Hitchcock, Nathaniel**
8/21/1746 3/9/1816
Nathaniel, Sr. was 1st settler in 1730. Home was at 603 Main St. Signed Non-consumption Pledge in 1774. A Nathaniel from Wilbraham enlisted in the Continental Army for 3 years and is credited with service in Major Lebbeus Ball's

Co., Col. William Shepard's Regt. from 2/25/77 - 12/31/1780 although memo in service records says he never served in the regiment. Other memos report that he was sick in the hospital on many occasions. Reported discharged 7/1/80. Residence also reported as Brimfield, Springfield and as Westfield, after 1777.

Hamp. **Hitchcock, Othniel**
8/10/1744 9/17/1807 63 Adams
Son of Lt. John. Marched on 4/20/75 with Capt. Paul Langdon in Col. Timothy Danielson's Regt. to Roxbury. Enlisted in to the army 4/29/75. Shows as corporal on muster rolls of 8/1 and 10/6. Named in letter of Dec. 75 from Capt. Langdon for "Bounty Coat".

Hitchcock, Perez
To Ticonderoga w/Capt. Daniel Cadwell. Enlisted 12/25/76, muster 2/24/77, Discharged 4/2/77 (99 days)

Hitchcock, Phineas
1/6/1761 - - d. Hebron, NY
With Capt. James Shaw at Bennington 9/24/77 - 10/18/77.

Wilb. **Hitchcock, Silas**
10/6/1739 - - d. New York
Brother of Nathaniel. Signed Non-consumption Pledge in 1774. Marched on 4/20/75 with Capt. Paul Langdon in Col. Timothy Danielson's Regt. to Roxbury. Did not enlist. Discharged 5/2/75. Served 12 days.

Wilb. **Hitchcock, Simeon**
9/23/1761 2/15/1840 78 d. New York
Enlisted for 3 months under resolve of 6/22/80. Age 18. In Capt. Joseph Browning's Co., Col. Seth Murray's Regt. 7/24/80 - 10/10/80. Son of Lt. John.

Hitchcock, William
To Ticonderoga w/Capt. Daniel Cadwell. Enlisted 12/25/76, muster 2/24/77, Discharged 4/2/77 (99 days). Enlisted for Wilbraham 11/28/81 for 3 years. Age 26, 5'6", light complexion, light hair, blue eyes, farmer.

Hodges, Eliphalet
In Capt. Abel King's Co., Col. Sears' Regt at Saratoga 8/20/81 - 11/20/81.

Houghton, Nathaniel -
Enlisted for Wilbraham (resolve of 6/9/79) for 9 months in Capt. Abel King's Co., Col. John Bliss's Regt. 7/18/79 - 4/18/80.

Howard, Aaron
With Capt. James Shaw at Bennington 9/24/77 - 10/18/77.

Howard, Benjamin
With Capt. James Shaw at Bennington 9/24/77 - 10/18/77.

Wilb. **Hubbard, David**
To Ticonderoga w/Capt. Daniel Cadwell. Enlisted 12/25/76, muster 2/24/77, Discharged 4/2/77 (99 days). Enlisted 7/18/80 for Springfield. In Capt. Joseph Browning's Co, Col. Moses Ashley's Regt at Camp Tenith (possibly Camp Totaway), NY. Discharged 12/8/80. Age 25, 5'9", light complexion, light hair, blue eyes, farmer.

Ludlow **Hubbard, Joseph**
Marched on 4/20/75 with Capt. Paul Langdon in Col. Timothy Danielson's Regt. to Roxbury. Did not enlist. Discharged 5/4/75, 14 days.

Huntley, John
Also Huntly. Enlisted for Wilbraham for 9 months. Arrived at Fishkill, NY, 7/20/78.

Irving, James, Jr.
Marched on 4/20/75 with Capt. Paul Langdon in Col. Timothy Danielson's Regt. to Roxbury. Did not enlist. Discharged 5/2/75, 12 days.

Ludlow **Jinnings, Joseph**
Marched on 4/20/75 with Capt. Paul Langdon in Col. Timothy Danielson's Regt. to Roxbury. Enlisted in to the army 4/29/75. Shows on muster rolls of 8/1 and 10/6. Named in letters in Dec. 75 from Capt. Langdon for "Bounty Coat". In Capt. Caleb Keep's Co, Col. Israel Chapin's Regt. 10/18/79 - 11/21/79 at Claverack for 3 mos.

Ludlow **Johnson, John**
Marched on 4/20/75 with Capt. Paul Langdon in Col. Timothy Danielson's Regt. to Roxbury. Enlisted in to the army 4/29/75. Shows on muster rolls of 8/1 and 10/6. Named in letters in Nov. 75 from Capt. Langdon for "Bounty Coat".

Wilb. **Johnson, Robert**
Also "Robbard Jonston" Enlisted for a class for Wilbraham for 3 years on 3/23/1781. Age 30, 5'5", dark complexion, dark hair, farmer.

Jones, Asa
6/12/1747 7/21/1820 73 -
With Capt. James Shaw at Bennington 9/24/77 - 10/18/77.

Taunton **Jones, John**
1757 3/1778 21 Adams
Signed Non-consumption Pledge in 1774. Capt. Josiah King's, Col. David Brewer's Regt. Enlisted 6/20/75. On muster rolls 8/1, 10/7/75 at Roxbury. Owed Bounty Coat, letter of 11/6/75. Letter for wages due Feb. - Aug. 76. In Capt. Moses Knap's Co., Col. Wm. Shepard's Regt. 1/1/77 - 3/78. Reported killed at Quebec, 3/78. Served for Taunton, buried in Wilbraham.

Jones, Joshua
"Jos'h". Marched on the Lexington Alarm of 4/20/75. Served 10 days.

Jones, Thomas Lt
1739 2/14/1825 86 Adams
One of the committee of three who picked the site for the first church. Signed Non-consumption Pledge in 1774. Marched with Paul Langdon to Roxbury 4/20/75. Discharged 5/5/75 - 15 days. Supposedly built the house at 200 Main St in Wilbraham in 1755, but this is unlikely as he would have been only 16 years old then.

Jones, Zenas
- 10/29/1780(?) 40 Adams
Signed Non-consumption Pledge in 1774. Marched with Paul Langdon to Roxbury 4/20/75. Discharged 6/6/75, 49 days.

Spgfld. **Keep, Matthew**
Marched to Roxbury 4/20/75 with Major Andrew Colton's Co. Service through 5/4/75 (15 days). With Capt. James Shaw at Bennington 9/24/77 - 10/18/77.

\- **Kibbe, Gideon** Capt
Signed Non-consumption Pledge in 1774. 12th (Hamp.) Co. Served in Capt Phineas Stebbins Co and as LT in Capt Samuel Burt's Co, Col Elisha Porter's Regt. Subaltern prior to May '76. 2LT til 1771. LT 1771-1781. 1781 + Captain. Commissioned Captain on 6/21/76.

\- **Kindal, Jacob**
To Ticonderoga w/Capt. Daniel Cadwell. Enlisted 12/25/76, muster 2/24/77, Discharged 4/2/77 (99 days)

Hamp. **King, Abel** LTC
\- 4/18/1812 69 -
Signed Non-consumption Pledge in 1774. 2LT in Capt. Cadwell's 7th Co. - Commissioned on 6/13/1776. Was Captain 7/16/79 (commissioned 12/22/79) at least through 4/16/80. Captain in Col. Sears' Regt at Saratoga 7/23/81 - 11/20/81. LTC 1782 - 1787. Marched on the Lexington Alarm of 4/20/75. Lived around 500 Glendale Rd, Hamp..

Wilb. **King, Asaph** Lt
1747 10/19/1834 88 Adams
From S.A.R. records. Listed as a forager under Capt. Abel King in 1778. Appointed Asst. Forage Master as a Lieutenant. Letter from 1782 for payment of wages assigned him for Joseph Cutt. Served in Rhode Island campaign. Granted pension at age 86. Born in Enfield. Sheriff during Shays Rebellion.

Hamp. **King, Luther** Fifer
3/22/1755 2/7/1784 28 -
Capt. Isaac Colton's Co., Col. David Brewer's Regt. Enlisted 5/10/75 at Roxbury. On 10/7 muster roll. Owed Bounty Coat, letter of 12/2/75. Son of William King. Lived at 43 North Rd, Hampden, in 1793.

\- **King, Oliver** Lt
With Capt. James Shaw at Bennington 9/24/77 - 10/18/77.

Hamp. **King, Solomon** Pvt
2/17/1748 9/28/1775 27 -
Signed Non-consumption Pledge in 1774. Capt. Isaac Colton's Co., Col. David Brewer's Regt. Enlisted 5/10/75. Died in camp at Roxbury.

Wilb. **King, Thomas** 2Lt
Signed Non-consumption Pledge in 1774. Sgt. on the Lexington Alarm of 4/20/75. Served 10 days. 2Lt in Capt. James Shaw's Company of Mattrosses, commissioned 9/11/76.

Hamp. **King, William** 1Lt
1724 - - -
William Jr. in F&I War at Crown Point in Oct. 1755 under Capt. Samuel Miller. Church records as Sgt in 1760. Ensign in new Co. formed 7/29/1774. Signed Non-consumption Pledge in 1774. Promoted to LT 4/20/1775. 1LT Jan 1776. Commander of 7th Co May 1776. Goat Rocks in Hamp. named so because his goats played there and one was found dead. Owned at least 86-180 Glendale Rd and most of Main St in Hamp.. Marched on the Lexington Alarm of 4/20/75. Served 10 days. Born in Palmer.

Bolton, CT **Ladd, Elisha**
1753 1840 - -
At Lexington for Bolton, CT. Born in Tolland, CT. Died in South Wilbraham (Hampden).

- **Lamb, Gad** Sgt
4/3/1739 - - -
Another Gad Lamb born in Wilb 9/5/1743 and also 1/9/44. Also, see Springfield Records.

Spgfld. **Lamberton, James**
To Ticonderoga w/Capt. Daniel Cadwell. Enlisted 12/25/76, muster 2/24/77, Discharged 4/2/77 (99 days). Sent to Ft. George with smallpox 2/8/77. Under Capt. John Morgan 1/9/78 - 7/1/78 to guard stores in Springfield and Brookfield. In Capt. Joseph Browning's Co., Col. Seth Murray's Regt 7/15/80 - 10/10/80 (3 months.).

Wilb. **Lampear, Jesse**
Wilb Baptist Church member. Also spelled Lamphere, Lampheare, Lamphire. Signed Non-consumption Pledge in 1774. To Ticonderoga w/Capt. Daniel Cadwell. Enlisted 12/25/76, muster 2/24/77, Discharged 4/2/77 (99 days).

Enlisted 9/24/77 for Bennington Alarm under Capt. James Shaw. Discharged 10/18/77 (32 days, 140 miles travel).

Wilb. **Lamson, William**
Capt. Charles Colton's Co., Col. Greaton's 3rd Regt. Enlisted 8/20/1777. 5'4" tall, Light Complexion. Dark Hair, Dark eyes. Paid 4,10,0. Deserted 11/1/1777.

Hamp. **Langdon, James**
3/27/1762 1804 - -
Served three months in Capt. John Carpenter's Guards at Springfield 7/13/79 - 10/8/79. In Capt. Joseph Browning's Co., Col. Seth Murray's Regt 7/24/80 - 10/10/80 (3 months) under resolve of 6/22/80.

Hamp. **Langdon, John** Sgt
6/1/1728 10/10/1822 94 Hampden
Crown Point 1755. Signed Non-consumption Pledge in 1774. Brother of Capt. Paul, father of John W. John W. was in same company at Roxbury with father and under Capt. Paul, his uncle. Letter from John at Roxbury refers to John (apparently his son) being well. Marched to Roxbury on 4/22/75 (after company). Enlisted 4/49/75 into army. On 8/1, 10/6 muster rolls in Roxbury and in Bounty coat letter of 12/23/75. D.A.R. says he raised a company of his own in Jackson's Regiment but this is wrong. That John Langdon was related, but was not this John. Possibly John, or his son John W. served under Capt. Aaron Graves, Col. David Leonard, 5/8/77 - 7/8/77 northward and with Capt Samuel Burt, Col. Elisha Porter, 7/22/79 - 8/25/79 at New London

Hamp. **Langdon, John Wilson**
3/11/1759 1842 - (d. Ohio)
Signed Non-consumption Pledge in 1774. At Roxbury in same company with his father John. Company was commanded by his uncle Paul. Marched 4/20/75. Enlisted 4/29. Muster roll of 10/6/75. Bounty coat letter of 12/25/75. Also, enlisted 9/24/77 for Bennington Alarm under Capt. James Shaw. Discharged 10/18/77 (32 days, 140 miles travel). Became superintendent of the powder works in Springfield. Died in Hamilton County, Ohio.

Hamp. **Langdon, Josiah**
1/2/1765 2/5/1855 90 Hampden

D.A.R. says at Lexington with his Uncle Paul, but unlikely as he would have been 10, and no state records as well. In Capt. John Carpenter's Guards at Springfield 2/1/81 - 4/1/81, raised for 8 months but only served two.

Hamp. **Langdon, Lewis**
6/15/1749 1829 - -
Lived at 16 Somers Rd, Hampden, at one time. Father (Paul) owned first sawmill in town in 1750. Signed Non-consumption Pledge in 1774. Marched on 4/20/75 with Capt. Paul Langdon in Col. Timothy Danielson's Regt. to Roxbury. Did not enlist. Returned home 5/8/75. Appointed to committee of three to look after families of those away at war. At Fishkill and Claverack, NY, 10/18/79 - 11/21/79 in Capt. Caleb Keep's Co., Col. Israel Chapin's Regt. 6' tall, dark complexion. Also, 6/16/78 for 9 months, under resolve of 4/20/78 possibly under Capt. Stebbins, Col. Bliss's Regt.

Hamp. **Langdon, Paul** Captain
12/16/1725 6/23/1804 79 Hamp.
Served in pre-revolutionary years - see Colonial Period. Signed Non-consumption Pledge in 1774. Lieutenant in new Co. formed 7/29/1774. Promoted to Captain in March 1775. Son of Lt Paul Langdon. Lived at 128 Somers Rd, Hampden, in 1777. Captain of 12th Co (Hamp. Co.) throughout 1776.

Hamp. **Langdon, Philip**
8/22/1759 8/31/1853 94 Indiana
Capt. Joseph Browning's Co., Col. Seth Murray's Regt. 3 months under resolve of 6/22/80 (7/24/80 - 10/10/80) at age 21. Died in Washington County, Indiana.

\- **Leach, Jonathan**
\- 6/1/1780 37 -
Also Leech. With Capt. James Shaw at Bennington 9/24/77 - 10/18/77.

\- **Leach, Joshua**
\- 1776 - -
This is very likely the man listed in State records as "John Leech" who died on board the galley "Trumbell" in October 1776 during the Lake Champlain Expedition. He is referenced in a letter from his wife Susanna asking for aid

for herself and two small children as compensation for his death.

Sherburne **Learned, Samuel**
6/7/1756 12/4/1833 - -
In Capt. Amos Perry's Co., Col. Hawes' Regt at Rhode Island, 7/28/78 - 9/12/78. Also drafted for 6 months for Sherburne beginning 7/7/80. Born in Framingham, died in Wilbraham (DAR)

Hardwick **Leonard, Ezra** Ensign
1711 6/29/1798 87 Hampden
Committee of Safety in Hardwick, MA, in 1774. At Lexington with Capt. Edmond Hodges. Service on 4/23/81. Born in Marlboro, MA. Died in Wilbraham.

- **Lewis, Isaac**
- 11/21/1847 91 -
"Soldier of the Revolution". Isaac Lewis from Ashfield, Deerfield, and Westfield served in Revolution. Can't tell which one this is. Died in Wilbraham.

Wilb. **Lillie, Emmons**
1764 - - d. in Bethel, VT
Son of Obadiah. Under the resolve of 6/5/80, served 6 months (7/3/80 – 1/5/81) at West Point in Capt. Daniel's Co., 6th Mass. Regt. Age 20, 5'8', Ruddy complexion.

Wilb. **Lillie, Nathan**
Also Lilley. 6/5/80 resolve. Age 21, 5'8", light complexion. For Wilbraham. Capt. Luke Day's Co., LTC John Brooks Regt 7/28/80 - 1/27/81 for 6 mos

Wilb. **Lillie, Obadiah**
7/17/1733
Also Lilley. Six months for Wilb. 7/27/80 - 1/27/81. Enlisted for Wilbraham 4/4/81 for 3 years. Age 45, 5'7" dark complexion, dark hair. Farmer. Born at Stafford, CT.

Wilb. **Lillie, Samuel**
Also Lelly, Lilley. Bounty 11/12/81 for a class paid John Shaw for Wilbraham for 3 years.

- **Loomis, Solomon**
Possibly this is Solomon, b. 1755 in Lebanon, CT who married Lucy Colton of Longmeadow. To Ticonderoga

w/Capt. Daniel Cadwell. Enlisted 12/25/76, muster 2/24/77, Discharged 4/2/77 (99 days).

- **Lothrop, Solomon**
With Capt. James Shaw at Bennington 9/24/77 - 10/18/77. Could be the son of Jonathan & Susannah of Bridgewater, MA (then b. 2/9/1761 d. 10/19/1843) or the son of Rev. Joseph of West Springfield (then b. 3/27/1760 d. 4/27/1787).

Ludlow **Lumbard, Jonathan**
- 1838 77 Ludlow
3 months for Wilb. 9/15/78 - 12/12/78 under Capt Phineas Stebbins, Col. Nathan Sparhawk. 9 months service for Ludlow in Capt. Miller's Co., Col. Bliss's Hampshire Regt 8/4/79 - 5/1/80. Age 17, 5'4", Brown hair, Light complexion. Occupation Farmer. 6 Months for Ludlow 8/12/80 - 12/17/80. 3 years service enlisted by Capt. Langdon for Wilbraham starting 6/29/1781 at York Huts (Capt. Haskell, Col. Wm. Shepard's 4th Regt). Listed as AWOL Oct/Nov 1781.

Wilb. **Lyon, Philip** Sgt
1729 1811 - -
Marched on 4/20/75 with Capt. Paul Langdon in Col. Timothy Danielson's Regt. to Roxbury. Enlisted in to the army 4/29/75. Shows as sergeant on muster rolls of 8/1 and 10/6. Named in letter of Dec. 75 from Capt. Langdon for "Bounty Coat". In Capt. John Carpenter's Guards at Springfield 6/9/80 - 2/10/81 (8 months). Born in Woodstock (?), died in Ludlow.

Wilb. **Lyon, Samuel** Pvt
3/27/1752 7/23/1778 26 -
Another Samuel Lyon born 1/12/57. In 2nd Co., Col. Marshall's Regt. 3/9/77 - 7/23/78. Died 7/23/78.

- **Mann, Ephraim**
Under Captain Phineas Stebbins, Col. Nathan Sparhawk, 9/15/78 - 12/12/78, service at Boston.

Wilb. **Mason, Daniel**
Drafted for 6 months service 7/3/80 - 12/17/80 under the resolve of 6/5/80. Age 19, 5'7", light complexion. In Capt. Abel Holden's Co., Col. Thomas Nixon's Regt at West Point.

Corporal in Capt. Abel King's Co., Col. Sears' Regt at Saratoga 8/20/81 - 11/20/81.

Wilb. **Mason, Phineas** Pvt
Enlisted for 3 years in Capt. Sizer's Co., Col. Jedutha Baldwin's Regt. 3/12/1778. Deserted 11/16/1779.

\- **McElwain, John** Sgt
Also sp. McElwein. To Ticonderoga w/Capt. Daniel Cadwell. Enlisted 12/25/76, muster 2/24/77. Sent to Ft. George with smallpox 2/1/77. Also in petition for expenses due to smallpox (See Daniel Cadwell). Discharged 4/2/77.

\- **McMaster, Robert** 2Lt
To Ticonderoga w/Capt. Daniel Cadwell. Enlisted 12/25/76. Sent to Ft. George with smallpox 2/13/77. Also in petition for expenses due to smallpox (See Daniel Cadwell). Discharged 4/2/77.

Wilb. **Merrick, Caesar**
\- - - Adams
Generally spelled as Mirick. Believed to be one of David Merrick's slaves. Listed as "a negro" in Capt. J. Woodbridge's Company, Col. Tyler's Regiment. Enlisted 7/3/79 - 11/15/79 at Rhode Island. Also, under the resolve of 6/22/80, for 3 months in Capt. Joseph Browning's Co., Col. Seth Murray's Regt 7/24/80 - 10/10/80 (Cont. Army). Enlisted at age 45.

Wilb. **Merrick, Chileab**
5/1749 5/1/1833 84 Adams
Deacon. Son of Rev. Noah, brother of Samuel F. Marched on the Lexington Alarm of 4/20/75. Served 10 days.

\- **Merrick, George**
\- 1776 - -
According to town records he died in the Army of Canada in 1776, but this is not listed in the state records.

Wilb. **Merrick, Jonathan** Lt
3/21/1747 3/31/1812 65 Adams
Son of Deacon David Merrick. Cousin of Samuel F. Married his cousin Mary, daughter of Lt. Thomas. Enlisted 9/24/77 for Bennington Alarm under Capt. James Shaw. Discharged 10/18/77. Possibly other service for 15 days in July 1778

in Col. Jacob Gerrish's Regiment of Guards. Still listed as a Lieutenant on town records in 1782.

Wilb. **Merrick, Samuel Fiske** Pvt/Surgeon
9/13/1751 7/22/1836 84 Adams
Doctor. Marched on the Lexington Alarm of 4/20/75. Served 10 days. Served with "Army of Canada" late 1776. Enlisted 9/24/77 for Bennington Alarm under Capt. James Shaw. Discharged 10/18/77. Town Clerk 1786-90. Rev. War Pension $246.66/yr. Died 9/2/1835. Son of Rev. Noah Merrick. Constitutional Convention delegate in 1779. Justice of the Peace 1814. Author of Wilbraham Historical Address in 1813. Numerous other town contributions. Also, see journal and letter.

Wilb. **Mighets, Nathaniel**
Also Mighels. Marched on 4/20/75 with Capt. Paul Langdon in Col. Timothy Danielson's Regt. to Roxbury. Enlisted in to the army 4/29/75. Shows on muster rolls of 8/1 and 10/6. Named in letters in Dec. 75/Jan. 76 from Capt. Langdon for "Bounty Coat".

\- **Miller, William**
Paid bounty by Moses Burt by a "class" for 3 year enlistment for Wilbraham. Age 17, 5'1" light complexion, light hair, farmer. Enlisted 3/26/81. Reported as unfit for duty - undersize.

Spgfld **Mills, James**
Enlisted for 9 months for Wilbraham from time of arrival at Fishkill under resolve of 4/20/78. Age 18, 5'5", dark comp. Brown hair. In Capt. Stebbins' Co., Col. John Bliss's Regt. Arrived at Fishkill on 6/16/78.

Palmer **Moore, Judah** fifer
Fifer for Capt. Rueben Munn's Co, Col. Nicholas Dikes' Regt 11/26/76. Drummer for Capt. Caldwell. Fifer under Lt. Joshua Shaw 9/26/77 - 10/18/77 (29 days).

\- **Morris, Chester**
In Capt. John Carpenter's Guards at Springfield 2/3/81 - 4/1/81 (3 months, enlisted for 8).

Hamp. **Morris, Edward**
12/12/1756 4/29/1801 45 Hampden

Enlisted 9/24/77 for Bennington Alarm under Capt. James Shaw. Discharged 10/18/77. In Capt. Caleb Keep's Co., Col. Israel Chapen's Regt. At Claverack 10/18/79 - 11/21/79 (3 months, Cont. Army). D.A.R. records show him in Canada under Gen. Thomas. Born in Woodstock, CT.

Hamp. **Morris, Isaac**
1753 6/26/1805 53 Hampden
Marched on the Lexington Alarm of 4/20/75. Served 10 days.To Ticonderoga w/Capt. Daniel Cadwell. Enlisted 12/25/76, muster 2/24/77, Discharged 4/2/77 (99 days). Enlisted 9/24/77 for Bennington Alarm under Capt. James Shaw. Discharged 10/18/77. Served under Capt Theophilus Munson 1/1/78 - 1/10/78. Born in Woodstock, CT.

Hamp. **Morris, Joseph**
- 8/10/1776 22 Hampden
Died at Lake George "in service to his country". No record of this in State records.

- **Murphy, Timothy**
To Ticonderoga w/Capt. Daniel Cadwell. Enlisted 12/25/76, muster 2/24/77, Discharged 4/2/77 (99 days)

Monson **Newell, Abijah**
1/9/1731 - - -
Not a Wilb. Soldier, but was father of Stephen Newell. Capt. Joshua Shaw's Co., Col. Elisha Porters Regt. 7/22/79 - 8/27/79 at New London. There is an Abijah Newell buried in Monson but he died at age 79, 8/28/1841. He would have been 17 in 1779, so unlikely to have a son as old as Stephen. Possibly this is Stephen's brother. Also, Abijah Newell from Monson enlisted in Capt. Abel King's Co. at Saratoga on 8/20/81 for 3 months (disch. 11/20/81). Also probably Stephen's brother.

Hamp. **Newell, Stephen** Fifer
6/71758 8/28/1848 90 Hamp.
Lived at 421 Glendale, Hampden, in 1795. Stephen was the son of Abijah who moved to Monson from Dudley in 1775. According to the Hamp. hostory, Abijah was drafted but was unable to serve because of his large family and offered his son Stephen as his replacement. Stephen served "faithfully and with courage." Based on State records, if this

is so, it would have been the service starting 7/24/80 for Monson as Abijah served only a month in 1779. Stephen, born in Dudley in 1758, was said to be eccentric in his later years. He predicted to the week his own death four years before he died and assisted in the digging and shoring up of his own grave. He also prepared his own tombstone, except for the date. Stephen died in 1848 while living at 25 Chapin Rd in Hamp.. Capt. Rueben Munn's (Monson) Co., Col. David Leonard's Regt. 3/1/77 - 4/11/77 at Ticonderoga. Also, enlisted for Monson 7/24/80 - 12/13/80. Age 22, 5'7", dark complexion. Possibly more service in 77 & 79.

Wilb. **Newton, Paul**
Capt. Isaac Colton's Co., Col. David Brewer's Regt. at Roxbury. Enlisted 5/10/75. Muster 8/1/75. Owed Bounty Coat in letter of 11/15/75.

\- **Newton, Phineas** Lt
\- 7/12/1779 72 Adams
Capt. John Morgan's Co., enlisted 1/3/78 - 7/1/78 to guard stores at Springfield and Brookfield.

\- **Oakes, Ebeneezer**
To Ticonderoga w/Capt. Daniel Cadwell. Enlisted 12/25/76, muster 2/24/77, Discharged 4/2/77 (99 days)

Wilb. **Orcutt, John**
Enlisted for 6 months under the resolve of 6/5/80 (7/28/80 - 12/21/80) age 28, 5'8", light complexion.

Spgfld **Osborn, Isaac**
9/19/1760 2/20/1843 82 Sherman, NY
Born in Wilbraham. Signed Non-consumption Pledge in 1774. Enlisted while residing in Springfield on 8/1/1776 as a private in Col. John Bliss' regt. Served until 1/1/1777. Enlisted July 1777 for 6 months in Capt. Enos Parker's company. Enlisted 1/1/1779 for three years as an artillery artificer in Capt. William Barton's Co., LTCol. David Mason's Regt in Springfield. Enlisted 1/8/1782 and served through 6/15/1783 as an artifcier in In Capt. Hawes' Co, Col. David Mason's Regt. Received pension in on 10/12/1832 while living in NY. Buried in Panama Cemtery, Harmony NY.

Wilb. **Osborn, William**
Also Osbon. Signed Non-consumption Pledge in 1774. Marched with Capt. Langdon 4/20/75. Served 11 days. Discharged 5/1/75. 3rd Regt. Enlisted 3/15/1777 in Capt. Charles Colton's Co., Col. John Greaton's Regt. 5'8" tall, Light Complexion. Light Hair, Light eyes. 43 years old. Paid 4,10,0. Deserted.

\- **Palmer, Elijah**
To Ticonderoga w/Capt. Daniel Cadwell. Enlisted 12/25/76, muster 2/24/77, Discharged 4/2/77 (99 days)

\- **Parsons, Daniel** 1Lt
Capt. Walter Pynchon's Co., 1st Hampshire, on 5/21/76, commissioned 6/13/76. To Ticonderoga w/Capt. Daniel Cadwell. Enlisted 12/25/76, muster 2/24/77, Discharged 4/2/77 (99 days). Also Capt. John Carpenter's Guards 3/11/79 - 6/11/79 at Springfield.

Wilb. **Parsons, Elijah**
4/17/1744 5/5/1796 52 -
In State records as Persons. Signed Non-consumption Pledge in 1774. Marched with Capt. Langdon, did not enlist. Served 4/20/75 to 5/2/75 (12 days).With Capt. James Shaw at Bennington 9/24/77 - 10/18/77. Married Capt. Daniel Cadwell's sister Eunice.

Glouc. **Parsons, Joshua**
Possibly from Gloucester, Mass. Did not march, but served at Ticonderoga w/Capt. Daniel Cadwell. Enlisted 2/14/77, muster 2/24/77, Discharged 4/2/77 (48 days)

Wilb. **Partridge, Deuty**
\- 4/10/1818 65 Glendale
Lived on Glendale Rd just north of Monson Rd in Wilbraham. "Duty Patrig" served in Capt. Joseph Cutler's Co. of Volunteers in the Northern Dept. The company marched on 9/24/77 from Warren, MA.

Somers **Pease, Joel**
11/2/1760 - -
Enlisted 7/10/81 in a "class" for Wilbraham for 3 years. Age 20, 5'8", Light complexion and hair. Farmer. Became Captain of Somers, CT militia

- **Percival, Gordin**
"Gordon Perival" With Capt. James Shaw at Bennington 9/24/77 - 10/18/77.

- **Percival, Jabez**
1760 1841 - -
In Capt. Abel King's Co., Col. Sears Regt 8/20/81 - 11/20/81 at Saratoga. Born in Middlesex, CT. Died in Lawrenceburg, IN.

- **Polley, Jonathan**
Drafted for 8 months, 6/15/78 for service at Fishkill, NY, in Col. Greaton's Regt.

- **Raymond, John** Cpl
Also Rayment and Raymont. Served all three years of enlistment. 3rd Regt. Enlisted 3/1/1777. In Lt. Col's Co., Col. Greaton's Regt. 1/1/80 - 3/1/80. 5"7" tall, Dark Complexion. Dark Hair, Dark eyes. 23 years old. Paid 4,10,0.

- **Richardson, James**
Capt. John Carpenter's Guards at Springfield 3/5/81 - 5/1/81 (enl. for 8 mo's).

- **Richardson, Johnson**
Capt. John Carpenter's Guards at Springfield 12/6/80 - 4/16/81.

- **Rogers, Jonathan**
At Ticonderoga w/Capt. Daniel Cadwell (did not initially march with unit). Enlisted 1/12/77, Discharged 4/2/77 (81 days)

Monson? **Rogers, Nathaniel**
Possibly from Monson. To Ticonderoga w/Capt. Daniel Cadwell. Enlisted 12/25/76, muster 2/24/77, Discharged 4/2/77 (99 days). Also served under John Bliss.

Hamp. **Rood, Moses**
Wilb Baptist Church. Marched on 4/20/75 with Capt. Paul Langdon in Col. Timothy Danielson's Regt. to Roxbury. Enlisted in to the army 4/29/75. Shows on muster rolls of 8/1 and 10/6. Named in letters in Dec. 75/Jan. 76 from Capt. Langdon for "Bounty Coat".

N'Hamptn **Root, Timothy**
Also Roott. To Ticonderoga w/Capt. Daniel Cadwell. Enlisted 12/25/76, muster 2/24/77, Discharged 4/2/77 (99 days)

Hamp. **Russell, Benjamin**
1759 1776 16 -
To Ticonderoga w/Capt. Daniel Cadwell. Enlisted 12/25/76, muster 2/24/77, Discharged 4/2/77 (99 days), Died at Ticonderoga. Stebbins say born 1762 and died at age 16. No State records.

Hamp. **Russell, Ezekiel** Sgt
1721 1/3/1802 80 Hampden
Born at Reading, MA. Moved to Hamp. at 192 North Rd in 1759. Signed Non-consumption Pledge in 1774. Marched at Lexington. Sgt in Capt. Phineas Stebbins' Co., Col. Nathan Sparhawks Regt 9/15/78 - 12/12/78 at Boston.

Wilb. **Russell, John** Cpl
- 5/23/1839 84 Adams
Records say Corporal but gravestone says Lieutenant, possibly militia officer after rev. war. Capt. Rueben Munn's Co., Col. Nicholas Dike's Regt. At Roxbury at least from 9/17/76 - 11/26/76. Enlisted for Wilbraham at Fishkill, NY, 6/9/78.

Hamp. **Russell, Robert**
- 1/9/1836 79 Hampden
Capt. Samuel Burt's Co., Col. Porter's Regt. 7/22/79 - 8/25/79 at New London.

Conn. ? **Scales, John**
- 11/24/77 - -
No information except a "soldier of Willimantic". This was likely a Connecticut solider guarding Burgoyne's troops on their march through Wilbraham following Saratoga.

- **Searles, Joshua**
To Ticonderoga w/Capt. Daniel Cadwell. Enlisted 12/25/76, muster 2/24/77, Discharged 4/2/77 (99 days)

Hamp. **Sessions, Robert, Jr.** Lt
3/15/1752 9/27/1836 84 Hampden
Moved to Boston as a young man and was at Boston Tea Party. Afterwards he fled the city and returned to Pomfret.

He had four brothers who fought in the Revolution. At Lexington in Capt. Ingall's Co., Col. Williams' Regt. D.A.R. says he was a "Pvt, Sgt, & Lt of CT militia in Rhode Island in 1776/7". Born in Pomfret, CT. Moved to Wilbraham in 1781. Received Hamp. Cty Pension. Town Clerk 1793 - 1805. Lived at 625 Main St, Hampden, at one time and at 300 Wilbraham Rd in 1781. Justice of the Peace 1814.

Hamp. **Sexton, Joseph** Sgt
Hannah, wife of Ensign Jos. Sexton at Hamp. (5/26/1784, 80). With Capt. Shaw at Bennington.

Wilb. **Sexton, Oliver Chapin**
1759 1845 -
In Capt. J. Woodbridge's Company, Col. Tyler's Regiment 7/22/79 - 12/25/79 at Newport, RI. Born in Wilbraham. Died in Lambertville, MI.

Hamp. **Sexton, Samuel** 1LT
- 3/22/1816 - -
Also given as Saxton. Son of Ezekiel. Lived at 241 North Rd, Hampden, in 1792. Signed Non-consumption Pledge in 1774. James Shaw's Artillery Co., Col. Pynchon's Regt. Commissioned 9/11/76. He is later referred to as Captain in 1777, but I could find no records corresponding to this promotion in the state records.

Wilb. **Shaw, James** Captain
- 4/8/1831 92 Adams
Enl 5/5/1775, LT in June. Son of James Shaw (2Lt) at Cape Breton. Captain of Company of Mattrosses (artillery) in Col. Charles Pynchon's 1st Hampshire Regt., established 8/7/76, commissioned 9/11/76. Private with Cadwell at Ticonderoga. Reported with smallpox 2/15/77. Captain of Company sent on Bennington Alarm, 9/24/77 - 10/18/77.

Wilb. **Shaw, Knowles** Cpl
1758 1832 - -
Son of Capt. John Shaw. To Ticonderoga w/Capt. Daniel Cadwell. Enlisted 12/25/76. Sent to Ft George with smallpox 2/15/77. Mentioned in letter of 6/2/77 from father asking for expenses due to smallpox (see Daniel Caldwell letter). Also a Corporal in Capt. Samuel Burt's Co. Col. Elisha Porter's Regt, enlisted 7/22/79, discharged 8/25/79. Service at New London, CT. Died in Venice, OH.

-	**Shayler, Reuben** Possibly this is Rueben Thayer. Also in records as Shalyer. Marched on the Lexington Alarm of 4/20/75. Served 10 days. Enlisted in to the army with Capt. Langdon 5/24/75. Shows on muster rolls of 8/1 and 10/6. Named in letters in Jan. 76 from Capt. Langdon for "Bounty Coat".
Monson	**Shields, David L.** Captain - 5/8/1843 85 Adams Gravestone says he was one "who served during the whole revolutionary war and for eight months was imprisoned by the British. He lived a true patriot and an honored citizen of the country he fought and suffered to redeem." Served in Capt. Caleb Keep's Co., Col. William Shephard's (3rd) Regt. 4/1/77 - 12/31/79 for Monson. Taken prisoner on 12/28/77, rejoined 8/5/78 in LTC Ebeneezer Sprout's Co., same Regt. Transferred to Light Infantry under Capt. John Wright, same Regt. and served March and April 1779 at Providence, RI. Corporal in Capt. Webb's Co throughout 1780 at West Point. In Capt. David Holbrook's Co., through 1781, then promoted to sergeant for 1782 at the Hutts in NY.
Wilb.	**Sikes, John James** Also John Jones Sikes. 6 months service for Wilbraham under resolve of 6/5/80 (7/3/80 - 12/17/80) age 20, 5'9" light complexion. In Capt. Abel Holden's Co., Col. Thomas Nixon's Regt at West Point. Returned home after discharge with Daniel Mason.
Wilb.	**Sikes, Jonathan** Cpl 2/20/1748 - - - Signed Non-consumption Pledge in 1774. Marched on 4/20/75 with Capt. Paul Langdon in Col. Timothy Danielson's Regt. to Roxbury. Enlisted in to the army 4/29/75. Shows on muster roll of 8/1. Named in letters in Jan. 76 from Capt. Langdon for "Bounty Coat". Detached for service at Quebec in 1775. 3rd Regt. Enlisted 11/14/1776. 5'10" tall, Light Complexion. Dark Hair, Light eyes. 29 years old. Paid 4,10,0. Served in Capt. Colton's Co., Col. Greaton's Regt 1/1/77 - 11/14/79. Drafted as sgt 7/24/80 - 10/10/80 in Capt. Joseph Browning's Co., Col. Seth Murray's Regt. in Cont. Army.
Wilb.	**Sikes, Nathan** 1/4/1754 - - -

Marched on 4/20/75 with Capt. Paul Langdon in Col. Timothy Danielson's Regt. to Roxbury. Enlisted in to the army 4/29/75. Shows on muster rolls of 8/1 and 10/6. Named in letters in Dec. 75 from Capt. Langdon for "Bounty Coat". Also Capt. Summers' Co., Col Greaton's Regt 5/10/77 - 12/31/79. Colonel's Co, Col. Greaton's Regt. 1/1/80 - 5/10/80.

Wilb. **Simonds, Aaron**
Also Simons. Capt. Colton's Co., Col. Greaton's 3rd Regt. Enlisted 1/1/1777 for Wilbraham. 5'7" tall, Light Complexion. Dark Hair, Dark eyes. 20 years old. Paid 4,10,0. Discharged 12/31/79.

\- **Simonds, Asa**
With Capt. Shaw at Bennington.

Wilb. **Simons, Daniel**
Did not march on 4/20/75 with Capt. Langdon but with him at Roxbury. Enlisted in the army 5/8/75. Shows on muster rolls of 8/1. Named in letter in Jan. 76 from Capt. Langdon for "Bounty Coat".

Wilb. **Simons, Moses**
\- 2/1/1780 - -
Marched on 4/20/75 with Capt. Paul Langdon in Col. Timothy Danielson's Regt. to Roxbury. Enlisted in the army 4/29/75. Shows on muster rolls of 8/1 and 10/6. Named in letter in Dec. 75 from Capt. Langdon for "Bounty Coat". 3rd Regt. Enlisted 5/1/1777. 5'6" tall, Light Complexion. Light Hair, Light eyes. 21 years old. Paid 4,10,0. ('Symonds'). Capt. Charles Colton's Co., Col. Greaton's Regt. 5/1/77 - 2/1/80. Killed in 1780 at White Plains.

Wilb. **Simons, Stephen**
Enlisted under resolve of 6/5/80 in Capt. Moses Ashley's Co., Col. Joseph Vose's 1st Regt. 7/18/80 - 12/8/80 at Camp Tenith (near West Point, NY). Age 18, 5'4", dark complexion.

Hamp. **Skinner, Isaac**
\- 4/8/1782 - Hampden
"Killed by Indians not far from Little Falls" in local records, but no State records found.

-	**Smith, Eleaser** Signed Non-consumption Pledge in 1774. Marched on the Lexington Alarm of 4/20/75. Served 10 days.
Wilb.	**Smith, Ethan** Also known as Allen Smith. Capt. John Carpenter's Guards at Springfield 6/25/79 - 9/25/79 (3 months). Enlisted for six months on 8/1/80 under the resolve of 6/5/80 in Capt. Benjamin Heywood's Co., 6th Mass. Regt Cont. Army, discharged 12/18/80 at West Point. Age 17 5'9" Ruddy complexion.
Wilb.	**Smith, Henry** Hired by Jonathan Merrick (Mirick) and signed by Phineas Newton for a class on 4/5/81 to serve 3 years under the resolve of 12/2/80. Age 29, 5'9" light complexion, farmer, for Wilbraham. In Capt. Benjamin Warner's Co., LTC John Brooks' Regt at West Point on 4/2/81. Detached to Springfield Oct/Nov 81. Born in Great Britain, residence Wilbraham. Court martialed 1/27/82 for desertion. Sentenced to 100 lashes, pardoned. Court martialed 8/10/82, AWOL 2 days, 35 lashes. Deserted Nov. 1782.
Wilb.	**Smith, Ithamar** In Capt. Josiah Smith's Co., Col Josiah Whitney's Regt. For defense of Boston. Enlisted 5/25/76 for 6 months. Discharged 11/1/76.
-	**Smith, Luther** To Ticonderoga w/Capt. Daniel Cadwell. Enlisted 12/25/76, muster 2/24/77, Discharged 4/2/77 (99 days)
Ludlow	**Squire, Ezekiel** Marched on 4/20/75 with Capt. Paul Langdon in Col. Timothy Danielson's Regt. to Roxbury but did not enlist. Discharged 5/3/75 (13days). Also in Capt. Isaac Colton's Co., Col. David Brewer's Regt. 5/15/75 - 8/1/75.
Hamp.	**Stacy, Ebeneezer** 1752 10/25/1821 69 Hampden Lived at 211 South Rd, Hamp. Signed Non-consumption Pledge in 1774. Enlisted for town of New Salem, 7/19/79 for 9 months. Age 18, 5'4", brown hair. Also, Capt. Joseph Bates' Co., 14th Mass. Regt. 8/1/80 - 10/1/80.

Hamp. **Stacy, Simon**
Marched on 4/20/75 with Capt. Paul Langdon in Col. Timothy Danielson's Regt. to Roxbury. Enlisted in the army 5/4/75. Shows on muster rolls of 8/1 and 10/6. Named in letter in Dec. 75 from Capt. Langdon for "Bounty Coat". 9 months in Capt. Shaw's Co., Col. Bliss's Regt. Enlisted 10/19/79 for Monson. Age 25, 5'10", Red complexion, Red Hair.

\- **Steal, Joseph**
Marched on 4/20/75 under Maj. Andrew Colton. Served through 5/4/75, did not enlist in Cont. Army.To Ticonderoga w/Capt. Daniel Cadwell. Enlisted 12/25/76, muster 2/24/77, Discharged 4/2/77 (99 days). Marched with Capt. James Shaw at Bennington Alarm. Served 9/24/77 - 10/18/77.

Wilb. **Stearns, John**
1/11/1736 1788 - - -
1768 reference as a doctor. Marched on the Lexington Alarm of 4/20/75. Served 10 days. Possibly also under Capt. Wm. King in Dorchester on 11/17/75 (owed a "Bounty Coat"). 3 children buried at Adams Cem (Doc. John and Elisabeth Sterns"). Moved to Tolland after the war based on his sympathy with the men of Shay's Rebellion.

Hamp. **Stebbins, Aaron, 2nd** Cpl
3/20/1750 2/1/1819(?) 69? -
Son of Sgt. Aaron. Lived at 94 Mountain Rd, Hampden, before 1788. Signed Non-consumption Pledge in 1774. Marched on 4/20/75 with Capt. Paul Langdon in Col. Timothy Danielson's Regt. to Roxbury. Enlisted in the army 4/29/75. Shows on muster rolls of 8/1 and 10/6. Named in letter in Dec. 75 from Capt. Langdon for "Bounty Coat". Marched with Capt. James Shaw at Bennington Alarm. Served 9/24/77 - 10/18/77.

Hamp. **Stebbins, Calvin** Fifer
7/30/1751 11/7/1825 74 Hampden
Signed Non-consumption Pledge in 1774. Served 8 days at Lexington Alarm with Capt. Warriner. Marched with Capt. James Shaw at Bennington Alarm. Served 9/24/77 - 10/18/77. Brother of Moses Stebbins. Lived at 789 Main St, Hampden.

Hamp. **Stebbins, David**
1760 1/21/1844 84 Hampden
3rd Lt under Capt. Enoch Chapin, Col. Jacob Gerrish's Regt of Guards. 7/20/78 - 12/31/78 (6 months). Detached from Hampshire militia to guard stores at Springfield and Brookfield.

Hamp. **Stebbins, Enos** Sgt
7/26/1740 - - -
Signed Non-consumption Pledge in 1774. Marched on the Lexington Alarm of 4/20/75. Served 10 days. Also, Capt. Nathan Rowle's Co. 7/1/78 for 6 months in Rhode Island. Discharged 1/1/79.

Wilb. **Stebbins, Gaius**
Capt. John Carpenter's Guards at Springfield 3/14/79 - 6/14/79. Also in Capt. J. Woodbridge's Company, Col. Tyler's Regiment 7/22/79 - 12/25/79 at Rhode Island. Drafted for Capt. Joseph Browning's Co., 7/1/80 - 1/18/81 under the resolve of 6/5/80. Age 16, 5'11", light complexion.

Wilb. **Stebbins, James**
1760 1846 - -
In Capt. Phineas Stebbins' Co., Col. Nathan Sparhawk's Regt. 9/15/78 - 12/12/78, ordered to Boston. Mustered under Col. Bliss for 3 months in 12th Co., 1st Hampshire on 7/24/1780 at age 21, in Capt. Jos. Browning's Co, Col. Seth Murray's Regt. Discharged 10/10/1780. 3 months service. Born in Wilbraham, Died in East Longmeadow.

Wilb. **Stebbins, Joel**
- 6/3/1800 49 Adams
Marched on 4/20/75 with Capt. Paul Langdon in Col. Timothy Danielson's Regt. to Roxbury but did not enlist. Discharged 5/3/75 (13days). Also in Capt. Ephraim Chapin's Co.Col. Woodbridge's Regt. 8/15/77 - 11/30/77 with Northern Army (Gen. Gates)

- **Stebbins, John**
At Ticonderoga w/Capt. Daniel Cadwell. Enlisted 12/25/76, muster 2/24/77, Discharged 4/2/77 (99 days). Possibly more service as there are several John Stebbins in the State records.

Spgfld. **Stebbins, Medad** Cpl
Marched 4/20/75 under Major Andrew Colton. Served until 5/4/75 and returned home. At Ticonderoga w/Capt. Daniel Cadwell as a corporal. Enlisted 12/25/76, muster 2/24/77, Discharged 4/2/77 (99 days). Marched with Capt. James Shaw at Bennington Alarm. Served 9/24/77 - 10/18/77.

Hamp. **Stebbins, Moses, 3rd**
May 1750 June 1828 78 Hampden
Brother of Calvin. Signed Non-consumption Pledge in 1774. To Ticonderoga w/Capt. Daniel Cadwell as a private. Enlisted 12/25/76, muster 2/24/77, Discharged 4/2/77 (99 days).

Hamp. **Stebbins, Noah** 1Lt
10/13/1741 9/24/1818 77 Adams
Signed Non-consumption Pledge in 1774. Marched on 4/20/75 as Sgt. with Capt. Paul Langdon in Col. Timothy Danielson's Regt. to Roxbury but did not enlist. Discharged 5/3/75 (13 days). 1LT under Capt. Phineas Stebbins, commissioned 6/21/76. Marched to Bennington under Capt. James Shaw 9/24/77 - 10/18/77. Detached 7/10/78 to Col. Wade in Providence and served until 10/17/78. Seems to have served throughout the conflict in some capacity at least until 10/17/78.

Hamp. **Stebbins, Phineas** Captain
5/19/1739 4/1/1807 68 Hampden
Signed Non-consumption Pledge in 1774. 2LT in Jan 1776. In May '76, South Co becomes 12th Co of 1st Hampshire. Becomes Captain of 12th on 6/21/1776. Representative to General Court in 1786. Brother of Zadock. Lived at 111 Scantic Rd, Hampden, in 1769.

Wilb. **Stebbins, Seth** Cpl
Capt. Josiah Smith's Co., Col. Josiah Whitney's Regt 5/25/76 - 8/1/76 for defense of Boston, also 8/1 - 11/1/76, last 49 days as Corporal. Also served on board the sloop "Betsey" to Falmouth, Casco Bay, as guards for cannon being shipped. There were 3 Seth Stebbins, one born in 1739, his brother in 1753, and their cousin in 1754. Can't tell which one this is.

Spgfld? **Stebbins, Thomas** MAJ
May have been from Springfield or Longmeadow. Captain of Company of 68 men raised in Wilbraham, Springfield, and

West Springfield for Roxbury, Return dated 1/18/1776 for Col. Learned's Continental Regt. Commissioned 2/1/76, became 2nd Major 10/3/1777 for Col. Bliss's Regt by House of Representatives. Commanded a company sent northward at the Bennington Alarm on 8/14/77.

Hamp. **Stebbins, Zadock** Cpl
8/12/1741 4/20/1832 91 -
Brother of Phineas. Lived at 1 South Rd, Hampden, in 1791. Signed Non-consumption Pledge in 1774. In Capt. Rueben Munn's Co (Monson), Col. Nicholas Dike's Regt at Roxbury 9/17/76 - 11/26/77. Detached to march to Bennington under Capt. James Shaw 9/24/77 - 10/18/77. In Capt. Samuel Burt's Co., Col. Elisha Porter's Regt at New London 7/22/79 - 8/25/79. Enlisted for 3 months under the resolve of 6/22/80 by Col. Bliss (7/24/80 - 10/10/80) as corporal in Capt. Joseph Browning's Co., Col. Seth Murray's Regt. Age 35.

\- **Stranton, Samuel**
Enlisted for Wilbraham on 6/29/81 for 3 years. Age 28, 5'7", dark complexion, shoemaker.

Wilb. **Sweetland, Benjamin** Fifer
Capt. Aaron Coe's Co., LTC Timothy Robinson's Regt. Muster roll at garrison at Ticonderoga dated 2/24/77. Enlisted 12/25/76 through 3/25/77. In Capt. Charles Colton's Co., Col. John Greaton's 3rd Regt. Enlisted 5/1/1777, discharged 12/31/79. 5'6" tall, Dark Complexion. Light Hair, Light eyes. 22 years old. Paid 4,10,0

Somers **Sweetland, Daniel**
Did not march on 4/20/75 with Capt. Langdon, but enlisted 5/8/75 for 3 months, 1 day. On muster roll of 10/6/75 at Roxbury. Detached to Quebec during 1775. John Langdon at Roxbury refers to Daniel and Jeriah (brothers?). In records also as Swetland. Also with Captain Shaw at Ticonderoga 9/24/77 - 10/18/77

Somers **Sweetland, Jeriah**
With Capt. Paul Langdon in Col. Timothy Danielson's Regt. to Roxbury, but did not march on 4/20. . Enlisted in the army 5/8/75. Shows on muster rolls of 8/1 and 10/6. Named in letter in Dec. 75 from Capt. Langdon for "Bounty

Coat".Did not march on 4/20. John Langdon at Roxbury refers to Daniel and Jeriah (brothers?). Service 72 days.

Wilb. **Thomas, Ebeneezer**
Signed Non-consumption Pledge in 1774. John Carpenter's Guards at Springfield 3/15/1779 - 6/15/79 and 6/16/79 - 9/30/79, also 1/1/80 - 4/1/80. Drafted for Wilbraham for 6 months 7/3/1780 under the resolve of 6/5/80. Age 29, 6', light complexion. Reported sick in hospital at Fishkill, NY, 7/28/80. Discharged 11/11/80. Surgeon's recommendation for discharge said Thomas was "totally unfit for duty and had never rendered any actual service." It was futher recommended "to the civil and military officers of any town where he might take up residence in the future that he be retained at home." Nonetheless, it appears he served again with Capt. Carpenter at Springfield 2/12/1781 to 5/5/1781, 5/1/81 - 9/30/81, 10/1/81 - 12/1/81 in a company of rejected recruits. Also, he served at Castle Island as a "rejected recruit" on fort duty from 4/1/83 to 6/30/83.

Wilb. **Thomas, James**
Enlisted for 3 months under resolve of 6/22/80. Age 19. In Capt. Joseph Browning's Co., Col. Seth Murray's Regt. 7/24/80 - 10/10/80.

Hamp. **Thwing, John**
In Capt. Joseph Browning's Company, Col. Murray's Regiment, 7/24/80 for 3 months under the resolve of 6/22/80 at age 18. Lived at 300 Wilbraham Rd, Hampden, at one time.

\- **Tinney, Josiah**
To Ticonderoga w/Capt. Daniel Cadwell. Enlisted 12/25/76, muster 2/24/77, Discharged 4/2/77 (99 days). Possibly from Conway, MA. If so, has more service for Conway.

Woburn(?) **Tylar, Jonathan**
To Ticonderoga w/Capt. Daniel Cadwell (did not march with company). Enlisted 1/12/77, Discharged 4/2/77. Detached to Lake George Landing.

\- **Walbridge, Joshua**
\- 3/8/1846 88 East Wilbraham

Gravestone says "A Soldier of the Revolution" and "Battle of Valley Forge" No Mass. State Records.

- **Warner, Daniel**
- 2/21/1807 40 -
Enlisted for 3 months under resolve of 6/22/80. Age 16. In Capt. Joseph Browning's Co., Col. Seth Murray's Regt. 7/15/80 - 10/10/80.

Wilb. **Warner, Jesse** Lt
10/15/1738 2/20/1784 46 Adams
Signed Non-consumption Pledge in 1774. Private at Lexington. Marched on the Lexington Alarm of 4/20/75. Served 10 days. 2 LT in Capt. Abel King's 7th Co., Col. Bliss's Regt. Comissioned 12/22/79. Also, Capt. Joseph Browning's Co., Col Seth Murray's Regt. 7/4/80 - 10/10/80.

Warner, Nathaniel Edward
- 1/24/1743 - -
Son of Samuel, Sr. Died in New Hadley. Warner book says died in 1769 but it is wrong as he served in the Revolution. Marched with Capt. James Shaw at Bennington Alarm. Served 9/24/77 - 10/18/77.

Wilb. **Warner, Phanuel**
6/19/1746 6/29/1776 30 Adams
Marched on 4/20/75 with Capt. Paul Langdon in Col. Timothy Danielson's Regt. to Roxbury. Enlisted in to the army 4/29/75. Shows on muster rolls of 8/1 and 10/6. Detached to Quebec in 1775. Named in letters in Jan. 76 from Capt. Langdon for "Bounty Coat". Died of smallpox at Crown Point. Son of Samuel, Sr.

Wilb. **Warner, Samuel, Jr.** Pvt
1/1/1734 12/14/1823 90 Adams
Signed Non-consumption Pledge in 1774. Marched on the Lexington Alarm of 4/20/75 with Capt. Paul Langdon, served 11 days. Son of Samuel, Sr. To Ticonderoga with Capt. Daniel Cadwell 12/25/76 - 4/2/77.

Wilb. **Warner, Seth** Pvt
12/2/1760 1845 - New York
Cont. Army for 6 months. Enlisted in Springfield under the resolve of 6/5/80 on 7/3/1780 in Capt. Benjamin Heywood's Co, 6th Mass. Regiment. Discharged 12/8/1780 at West Point. Enlisted at age 19. Was 5'7" tall, dark

complexion. Also served in Capt. John Carpenter's Company of Guards 3/15/1779 to 6/15/1779 stationed at Springfield. Pension given by Greene County, NY, in 1832. Born in Wilbraham. Died in Freehold, NY.

- **Warren, Aaron** Captain
History of Hampden County, listed as Hampden Rev War soldier. No other records found.

- **Warriner, Abner** Cpl
12/12/1752 4/16/1827 75 Adams
Signed Non-consumption Pledge in 1774. Marched as fifer on 4/20/75 with Capt. Paul Langdon in Col. Timothy Danielson's Regt. to Roxbury. Enlisted in the army 4/29/75. Shows on muster rolls of 8/1 and 10/6. Named in letter in Dec. 75 from Capt. Langdon for "Bounty Coat". To Ticonderoga as a corporal with Capt. Daniel Cadwell 12/25/76 - 4/2/77. Also 3rd Regt. Enlisted 4/1777. 5'10" tall, Dark Complexion. Dark Hair, Light eyes. 24 years old. Paid 4,10,0. Pensioner. Born in Springfield. Brother of Daniel and Noah, son of Moses.

South Hadley **Warriner, Daniel**
1/16/1756 8/27/77 21 -
Brother of Abner and Noah, son of Moses. Capt. Leonard's Co., Col. Woodbridge's Regt. At Cambridge 6/24/75. Owed Bounty Coat, order of 10/25/75. In 2nd Co., Col. Thomas Marshall's Regt. In NY, 1/1/77 - 8/27/77. Died at Albany 8/27/77.

Wilb. **Warriner, David**
Signed Non-consumption Pledge in 1774. Marched with Capt. Paul Langdon to Roxbury 4/20/75 - 5/2/75 (12 days) but did not enlist.

Wilb. **Warriner, Gad**
1/29/1762 - - -
Enlisted under the resolve of 6/5/80 in Capt. Abel Holden's 6th Regt (Light Infantry) 7/3/80 - 12/16/80. Probably more service, many Gad Warriners. Age 18, 6', light complexion.

Wilb. **Warriner, James** Captain
1725 6/29/1795 70 Adams
F&I War. Possibly born 1723 and died 1793. Born in Springfield. Replacement to Louisburg Exped at Cape Breton 6/23/1745. Signed Non-consumption Pledge in 1774.

Ensign in July 1774. Town Clerk 1773-78, 1781-85. Captain of Lexington men.

Wilb. **Warriner, Moses II**
Served in Capt. Aaron Graves' Co., Col. David Leonard's Regt. 5/8/77 – 7/8/77, 70 days at the Northward. Also, Capt. Nathan Rowle's Co., Col. John Jacobs Regt. 7/1/78 - 1/1/79. Six months at Rhode Island.

Wilb. **Warriner, Noah** Lt
10/27/1748 1/29/1797 49 Adams
Son of Moses, brother of Abner and Daniel. Signed Non-consumption Pledge in 1774. Marched as sergeant on 4/20/75 with Capt. Paul Langdon in Col. Timothy Danielson's Regt. to Roxbury. Enlisted in to the army 4/29/75. Shows on muster rolls of 8/1 and 10/6. Named in letter in Dec. 75 from Capt. Langdon for "Bounty Coat". Town Clerk 1779-80. 1st Lt in Capt. Cadwell's Co., commissioned 6/13/76. In Capt. Nathan Rowe's Co., Col. John Jacobs' Rgt. 7/1/78 - 1/1/79 at Rhode Island.

\- **Warriner, Reuben**
11/17/1756 - - -
Served under Capt. James Shaw at Bennington 9/24/77 - 10/18/77. Corporal in Capt. Abel King's Co., Col. Sears Regt. 8/20/81 - 11/20/81 at Saratoga.

\- **Warriner, Solomon**
8/16/1753 3/12/1816 63 Adams
Son of and served under Capt. James Shaw at Bennington 9/24/77 - 10/18/77. First town librarian (1/7/1782)

Wilb. **Washburn, Seth**
4/20-30 to Roxbury (9 days) with Capt. Paul Langdon but did not enlist..

\- **Waters, Aaron**
To Ticonderoga w/Capt. Daniel Cadwell. Enlisted 12/25/76, muster 2/24/77, Discharged 4/2/77 (99 days)

Wilb. **West, Francis**
Enlisted under the resolve of 6/22/80 in Capt. Joseph Browning's Co., Col. Seth Murray's Regt. 7/24/80 - 10/10/80 at age 16. Capt. Abel King's Co., Col. Sears' Regt 8/20/81 - 11/20/81 at Saratoga.

Hamp. **West, Stephen** Quartermaster
1759 4/17/1814 55 Hampden
In 1782 lived at 1 South Rd, Hampden, and at 667 Main St after 1784.

- **White, David**
Served under Capt. James Shaw at Bennington 9/24/77 - 10/18/77

- **White, John**
Enlisted for 6 months under resolve of 6/5/80. Age 25, 5'7", light complexion. Served from 7/6/80 to 12/16/80 at West Point in the 10th Mass. Regt.

- **White, Josiah**
- 1776 - -
No State records found.

- **White, Lewis**
To Ticonderoga w/Capt. Daniel Cadwell. Enlisted 12/25/76, muster 2/24/77, Discharged 4/2/77 (99 days)

- **Whitney, Lemuel**
Served under Capt. James Shaw at Bennington 9/24/77 - 10/18/77.

Wilb. **Wight, Ephraim** Sgt
Signed Non-consumption Pledge in 1774. With Capt. Paul Langdon in Col. Timothy Danielson's Regt. at Roxbury. Did not march on 4/20. Enlisted in the army 5/15/75. Served 2 months, 22 days. Named in letter in Jan. 76 from Capt. Langdon for "Bounty Coat".

Wilb. **Wight, Ephraim, Jr.**
Signed Non-consumption Pledge in 1774. With Capt. Paul Langdon in Col. Timothy Danielson's Regt. at Roxbury. Did not march on 4/20. Enlisted in the army 6/8/75. Served 1 months, 12 days. Named in letter in Jan. 76 from Capt. Langdon for "Bounty Coat".

- **Willey, Joel**
Also Willee. To Ticonderoga w/Capt. Daniel Cadwell. Enlisted 12/25/76, muster 2/24/77, Discharged 4/2/77 (99 days)

Wilb. **Willey, Judah**
4/23/1743 - - -
Lived on western end of Glendale Rd. in Wilbraham. Moved to Warren ("Western Reserve") after the war.

Wilb. **Williams, James**
Capt. Charles Colton's Co., Col. John Greaton's Regt, Enlisted 2/1/1777. 5'4" tall, Dark Complexion. Dark Hair, Light eyes. 33 years old. Paid 4,10,0. Deserted on 6/10/77.

Hamp. **Williams, John**
- 4/21/1791 79 Hampden
Served in Capt. John Carpenter's Company of Guards 3/20/1779 to 6/20/1779 stationed at Springfield.

\- **Wood, David**
To Ticonderoga w/Capt. Daniel Cadwell. Enlisted 12/25/76, muster 2/24/77, Discharged 4/2/77 (99 days). Served under Capt. James Shaw at Bennington 9/24/77 - 10/18/77.

Wilb. **Woodworth, Asa** Pvt
Enlisted May 77 for duration of the war. 3rd Co., Col Brooks' Regt. Cont. Army 5/5/78 - 12/31/79. Capt. Benj Warren's Co., Mar/Apr 79 at Cherry Valley & Ft. Alden. Capt. Warren's Co., Col Brooks' 7th Regt. 1/1/80 - 12/31/80 at age 19, 5'8", light complexion, dark hair, born in Coventry, CT, residence Wilbraham. Feb - Apr/81 detached at Easton., May/81 at "the Lines", Jun - Sep/81 with Col. Scammel. Oct/81 - Feb/82 at York Hutts. All near West Point. Furlough started 1/4/82 for 40 days. Court Martial 5/5/82 for returning from furlough 19 days late. Sentenced to 30 lashes, pardoned. Discharged 6/9/83.

\- **Woodworth, Daniel**
To Ticonderoga w/Capt. Daniel Cadwell. Enlisted 12/25/76, muster 2/24/77, Discharged 4/2/77 (99 days). 3 year enlistment beginning 4/1/77 in Capt. Charles Colton's Co., Col. John Greaton's Regt. Reported died on 3/14/80.

\- **Woodworth, David**
Capt. Charles Colton's Co., Col. John Greaton's Regt. (3rd Regt.). Enlisted 2/10/1777 - 12/31/79 for Wilbraham. 5'6" tall, Dark Complexion. Dark Hair, Light eyes. 17 years old. Paid 4,10,0.

Wilb. **Woodworth, Ezekiel**
Also served for Palmer, and Springfield. Capt. Charles Colton's Co., Col. John Greaton's Regt. (3rd Regt.). Enlisted 2/10/1777 - 12/31/79 for Wilbraham. 5'7" tall, Dark Complexion. Light Hair, Light eyes. 18 years old. Paid 4,10,0. Lt. Col's Co., Col. Greaton's Regt. 1/1/80 - 2/16/80.

\- **Worthington, Timothy**
Served under Capt. James Shaw at Bennington 9/24/77 - 10/18/77.

\- **Wright, Benjamin** Pvt
2/8/1747 - - -
Signed Non-consumption Pledge in 1774. Listed in town histories but no other information found.

Ludlow **Wright, Cyprian** Pvt
\- - - Ludlow
Also Right. Marched on 4/20/75 with Capt. Paul Langdon in Col. Timothy Danielson's Regt. to Roxbury. Enlisted in the army 4/29/75. Shows on muster rolls of 8/1 and 10/6.

Wilb. **Wright, David** Pvt
In Capt. John Carpenter's Guards at North River, NY, 7/18/78 - 1/27/79 (6 months). With Capt. Carpenter at Springfield 3/11/79 - 6/11/79. Enlisted 7/5/81 for three years for a class in Wilbraham under the resolve of 12/2/80.

\- **Wright, Ezekiel**
Wilb Baptist Church. Marched on the Lexington Alarm of 4/20/75. Served 10 days.

\- **Wright, Henry**
12/17/1756 - - -
Capt. Charles Colton's Co., Col. John Greaton's Regt. (3rd Regt.). Enlisted 2/10/1777 - 12/31/79. 5'8" tall, Light Complexion. Light Hair, Light eyes. 20 years old. Paid 4,10,0. Signed Non-consumption Pledge in 1774. Enlisted for Wilbraham for 6 months 7/27/80 as wagoner for Capt. Luke Day, LTC John Brooks 7th Regt. Discharged 12/16/80 by Baron Steuben at Richmond, VA.

- **Wright, Josiah**
  - 1776 - -
  No State records. Town records say he "died in the army."

- **Wright, Philip** Pvt
  No State records.

- **Wright, Solomon**
  1747 1807? - -
  Born in Hebron, CT. Lived in Wilbraham in 1807. In Capt. John Skinner's Co. at Stillwater for Burgoyne's surrender (D.A.R.). Not sure if he died in Wilbraham.

- **Wright, Stephen** Sgt
  - 2/28/1832 83 -
  To Ticonderoga w/Capt. Daniel Cadwell. Enlisted 12/25/76, muster 2/24/77, Discharged 4/2/77 (99 days)

Appendix G - Wilbraham Soldiers – Post-Revolution through 1840

- **Alden, Jonah, 3rd**
In Ludlow Independent Co. – 1842

-- **Bennett, Ralph**
7/21/1798 1821 23 Glendale
War of 1812. Possibly died in 1831.

-- **Blanchard, Amasa**
Fought in the Seminole War. Lived near Monson & Hollow Road.

-- **Bliss, Lorenzo** 2Lt
North Co. 4/26/1837

-- **Brewer, Isaac**
- 11/21/1809
Mustered Oct 24, H1837 in Springfield Artillery

-- **Burr, Phineas**
- 8/3/1820?
War of 1812.

Wilb. **Butler, Benjamin** LTC
5/3/1808 9/28/1896 88 E. Wilb.
Commissioned 3/11/1836. Was the last Commander of a Wilbraham militia company.

Wilb. **Cadwell, Stephen Jr.**
-- 8/18/1844 63 Glendale
War of 1812. Lived on Glendale Rd, Wilbraham

Hampden **Carpenter, John, Jr.** Captain
- 2/16/1839 83 Glendale
Lived at 585 Glendale Rd, Hampden. Militia Captain sometime between 1792-1812.

Hampden **Chaffee, Comfort, Jr.**

Served in the militia to put down Shays Rebellion. Militia Captain sometime between 1792 - 1812. Lived at 180 Glendale Rd, Hampden, in 1792.

-- **Chaffee, Edward W.**
- 1/27/1860 55 Hampden
Mustered Oct 24, H1837 in Springfield Artillery

-- **Chapin, Isaac**
- 10/8/1855 78 Glendale
War of 1812.

-- **Clark, William** Major
- 1/2/1853 79 Adams
In Cemetery, no other records

-- **Cleaveland, Highland**
Militia in 1838

-- **Cone, Carson K.** Adjutant
Commissioned 7/28/1838

Hampden **Cone, Matthew**
- 10/13/1839 72 Hampden
War of 1812.

Monson **Cross, Stephen Jr.**
6/26/1787 4/2/1833 55 East Wilb.
War of 1812.

Wilb. **Day, Alfred**
5/20/1794 7/13/1886 92 Minn.
Buried in Castle Rock, MN. War of 1812. Enlisted as a drummer in 1814 at Commercial Point (near Boston).

-- **Ellis, Benjamin**
Militia in 1838, In 1840 was in Light Inf of Longmeadow

-- **Firman, Richard D.** Captain
South Co. 1838-1840

-- **Flint, Levi** Captain
- 8/1/1828 51 Hampden
Not in Wilb Records, but in cemetery

-- **Fuller, Ephraim** Lt
- 12/9/1838 84 Adams
Not sure of military service

-- **Glover, Peletiah** Quartermaster
- 5/12/1877 63 Adams
Reverend, Qtrmstr on 7/28/1838

-- **Hancock, John** 1Lt
North Co. 1831-1836

-- **Hendrick, Otis M.** Major
Commissioned 4/4/1838

-- **Hitchcock, Eleazer**
2/3/1782 7/5/1864
Served for seven months in the War of 1812.

-- **Jones, Solomon**
War of 1812.

-- **Knowlton, Daniel** Captain
12/23/1738 - - Adams
Son of Col. Knowlton from Hartford, aide to George Washington. Daniel's daughter buried at Glendale (d. 1801). Marcus Perrin Knowlton, Daniel's descendant, became Chief Justice of the Massachusetts Supreme Court (abt 1900).

-- **Knowlton, Francis**
War of 1812.

Wilb. **Knowlton, Nathaniel**
1/7/1794
War of 1812

Wilb. **Knowlton, Phineas**

11/8/1800 10/1827 27
Died in the U.S.Navy

Wilb. **Lard, Almond** 1Lt
South Co. - 1834.

Wilb. **Lathrop, Joseph** Captain
12/24/1766 12/11/1831 67 Adams
Introduced Saxon sheep into town. Born in West Springfield. Was a State Representative from Wilbraham.

-- **Lathrop, Seth** Colonel
Brigade Commander 1831-1833. Probably the son of Seth & Mehitable Lathrop of Bridgewater, MA. If so, he was born 2/26/1765.

-- **Lyman, Joel M.**
War of 1812.

Wilb. **Merrick, Jonathan** Lt
-- 3/31/1812 65

-- **Moore, Sydney**
Mustered Oct 24, H1837 in Springfield Artillery

-- **Morgan, Philip** Lt
-- 6/11/1814 44

Hampden **Morris, Edward** Quartermaster
-- 8/17/1824 40 Hampden
War of 1812. From 1810-1814, was 1st Regt Quartermaster. Lived at 650 Main St, Hampden, about 1806.

Wilb. **Partridge, Thomas**
-- 10/25/1813 24 Glendale
War of 1812. Died at Sackets Harbor. Son of Deuty. Name on stone with Mother.

Wilb. **Potter, Philip P.** Captain
-- 12/31/1847 66 Adams

Captain of 7th Co. 4/26/1837. Last Captain of a Wilbraham militia.

Hampden **Sessions, Charles** Captain
-- 4/4/1849 61 Hampden
Died in 1842? Lived at 625 Main St at one time. Was Captain in Militia sometime between 1792 and 1812. Introduced Merino sheep into town.

-- **Sessions, Oscar R.** Paymaster
Commissioned 7/28/1838

Hampden **Sessions, Robert, Jr.**
-- 6/5/1863 80 Hampden
War of 1812. Lived at 112 North Rd, Hampden.

-- **Sikes, Reuben** LTC
In 1790 was Captain of North Co.. Became Regt Commander in 1796

-- **Stebbins, George** 2Lt
1838 – in South (Hampden) Co.

-- **Stebbins, Jackson Walter**
-- 8/8/1820
Mustered Oct 24, H1837 in Springfield Artillery. See Civil War as well.

-- **Warner, Azriel** Captain
8/28/1766 - - -
1st Reg. 1st Brigade, H4 Div. Mass. Militia Lieutenant 4/26/1799. Captain Aug. 1, H1803 until he resigned on April 30, H1805. Son of Samuel Warner, Sr.

-- **Warner, James** Captain
-- 5/28/1816 53

-- **Warriner, Solomon, Jr.** LTC
3/24/1788 - -
Became Lt. Colonel of 1st BDE, H4th Div, MVM. Served in War of 1812 in Boston.

--	**Webster, Marcus**			
	--	4/2/1839	38	Glendale
Hampden	**West, John**	Major		
	1793	7/12/1826	--	Hampden
	Lived at 721 Main St, Hampden.			
--	**Wood, Almond**			
	Mustered Oct 24, H1837 in Springfield Artillery			
--	**Work, John**	Lt		
	--	5/19/1818	59	Adams
	In Cemetery, no other records			

Appendix H - Early Wilbraham Deaths

Even the most casual reader of Wilbraham's history knows about Timothy Mirick's rattlesnake bite and the tragedy on Nine Mile Pond in which six young people drowned while sailing in 1799. While doing research for this book, I came across the Wilbraham Vital Statistics compiled by Chauncey Peck in 1911. The section in the vital statistics on deaths contained, if not vital, at least some interesting information, particularly in terms of the official "writings" describing some of them.

I have categorized the information I found interesting as follows:

Drownings – I have never considered Wilbraham to be much of a "water" town and was surprised at the number of drownings. There were twenty drownings in town between 1762 and 1833. In addition, Noah Merrick, son of the minister, drowned while studying at Cambridge. While six occurred all at once, this still leaves fourteen, which seems a large number considering the size of the early population.

- Noah Merrick — 1762 (at Cambridge)
- Jonathan Kilborn — 1770 (of Monson)
- "unknown" — 1778
- Jonathan Leach — 1780 – 37
- Elijah Butler — 1782 – "child"
- Two Russells — 1783 (of Springfield)
- Polly Warriner* — 4/29/1799 – 16
- Abigail Fiske* — 4/29/1799 – 16
- Gordon Bliss* — 4/29/1799 – 29
- Leonard Bliss* — 4/29/1799 – 22
- Asenath Bliss* — 4/29/1799 – 16
- Guy Johnson* — 4/29/1799 – 24 (of Tolland, CT)
- Merrick Cooley — 1801 - 5
- Daniel Warner — 1807 – 40
- Littleton Wood — 1809 – 6
- Walter Wakefield — 1829 – 21
- Orson Beebe — 1829 – 22 (Scantic)

- Phebe Ann Atchinson 1830 – 3
- William Gates 1831 - 2
- Wells Lathrop 1833 – 16

* - Nine Mile Pond incident. "The above Named Persons were all suddenly Drowned while sailing in a Pleasure Boat on Nine Mile Pond in this town at the Above Date."

Paupers – There were quite a few people listed (all but one of whom died between 1841 and 1843) as either "Town" or "State" paupers. I assume this meant they relied on the town for support. My guess is the State passed an act around 1840 that provided for the support of paupers. As the Vital Statistics only covers the period up to around 1843, I suspect there would be more listed in later years as well.

- Mary Dumbleton 1779 (an "old Crase Girl" (crazy?))
- Woodbridge Potter 1841
- Hannah Charles 1841
- Henry Brass 1842
- Lidia Cooley 1842
- John Amidon 1843
- Solomon Charles 1843

Suicides – It's not That bad a town!

- Zenas Cone 1818
- Joseph Allard 1830
- Ralph Bennett 1831

Murders – Maybe it is for some!

- Reuben Cadwell ?
- Marcus Lyon 1805*
- Leander Chapin 1840

* - Dominic Daley and James Halligan, Irishmen walking across New England in search of jobs, were wrongfully convicted and hanged for this murder in 1806. The

Mass these two received on the night before their execution was the first Catholic service performed in Western Massachusetts. The actual murderer confessed to his crime on his deathbed in 1808.

Executions – Who'd a thought?

- William Shaw of Palmer for murder 1776

Lightning – A better choice than some that follows next

- John Stebbins 1834
- "An Academy Student"

Miscellaneous

Timothy Mirick 8/7/1761
"By the Bite of a Rattel Snake, Being 22 years, two months and three Days old and vary near the point of marridge."

Lois Bartlett 1774 Age 25 (daughter of Moses)
"Dyed whilst we attended on her Father's funeril. Dyed that moment her father was nailed up in the coffin, on the Sabbath day."

Nathaniel Burt 1735
"Cut his throat July 13, 1735, and lived But Little better than one day"
Note: Can't tell if an accident or suicide.

Leander Chapin 1840
From a knife wound received "by the hand of Sylvanus Griswold."

Zenas Cone July 3, 1818 age 55
"Put a period to his existence by hanging himself to a bar-post near his own home."

Noah Ferry 1834 age 19
"Killed instantly by a falling tree limb"

Thomas Glover 1775

"Dyed Dec. 30th 1775 in his 88th year - - a bachildor Never was married."

Francis Gowand 1764
"Ded on the Road that Leads from Na'll Blisses to William Kings. Soposed to have a fit of the Apoplex he was found on Wensda 16th Day of May 1764."

Asa Jones 7/21/1820 age 73
"casually by falling into a well"

Isaiah Leach 1816
"killed by a log rolling from a sled."

Peley Mason 1764
"Dyed by gitting a been in its gullet." (Choked on a bean)

Unknown 1778
"thare was the Body of a man found in the River between Lodlo and Wilbraham and a Jury of inquest set on it and brought in was some Sarpent Laid on him was the casion of his Death 1778." (Bitten by a snake and drowned?)

Mehitable Newton 1765
"Dyed May 16, 1765 – she Being Better than 20 yrs. Of age – Being Crase till she Dyed." (Crazy?)

Elijah Parsons 12/22/1773 age 2 ½
"met with the misfortin of being Burnt in a small hut made of turf and foled yt his father had to lay in while be Burnt a pit of Coal. Sd Child was so Burnt that he Dyed Nex Day which was Dec. 22, 1773."

William Rindge 5/4/1839 age 48
"Death occasioned by falling froma barn scaffold."

Rusel (Russell)
"Thear was two young men Suns of ___ Rusel of Springfield Drowned on Friday, may 23rd, 1783."

William Shaw of Palmer 1770

"Executed for murder on Thursday the 13th Day of December, 1770."

Parmela Stevens 8/10/1840 age 29
"killed by falling across a Rail Road Track."

Jacob Kibbe of Monson 4/5/1766
Killed "By Raising of a hous for William Barnes, the sides of the hous fell."

Joseph Coot 1772(?)
"A Negrow man Dyed. January 15, 1772"
Note: This may be the father of Joseph Cutt, one of three black Revolutionary War soldiers who fought for Wilbraham.

William Simons 1765
"hed of a family in this town. Froas to Death agoin from Daniel Hitchcocks to his own hous on Saturday January 19th, 1765, and lay till Monday Before he was moved."

Walter Wakefield 1829 age 21
Drowned in the Scantic while fishing with Orson Beebe. "Beebe accidentally fell in, and being no swimmer, Wakefield flew to his assistance, and both perished together."

Sarah Warriner 1770 age 5 months
"This child smothered."

Appendix I – Wilbraham Trivia

One cannot do research about the early days in Wilbraham without running across interesting tidbits about the town itself. While not directly related to the military rolls, I found this information amusing.

The first potatoes were grown in town by Deacon Nathaniel Warner about 1754.

Lt. Paul Langdon brought the first wagon. By 1784, there were but two two-horse wagons!

Before the Revolutionary War, Kittridge Davis was the town daredevil and would stand on his head on the gin-pole at local barn raisings.

David Chapin brought the first rat into town in a sack of wool from Rhode Island (and let it live).

Capt. Charles Sessions introduced Merino Sheep into town. Saxon sheep were introduced by Capt. Joseph Lathrop.

The North East village was called "sodom" and the South Parish was "pokeham." The South Village was "the city."

The Goat Rocks were so called as being the favorite resort of William King's goats. These rocks are a ledge about thirty feet perpendicular to the road, at the south end of the North Mountains. Modern roadmaps and USGS topographical still indicate the Goat Rocks here.

Rocky Dundee was the name of the region south of Burt's Mill.

Pole Bridge Brook was so called from the first bridge built over it. It was also called Beaver Brook because the beavers had built a dam in it.

Twelve Mile Brook was so-named because it was 12 miles from Springfield and Nine Mile Pond was 9 miles from Springfield.

Rattlesnake Peak received its name because a rattlesnake was killed there.

Wigwam Hill was named for the Indian Squaw's wigwam near it.

Stony Hill Road got its name because it was stony.

Peggy's Dipping Hole (now Dipping Hole Rd.) is called that because Peggy, in her desire to attend church in Springfield, ventured to cross some recently frozen ice and went through into the water (according to one local legend).

Wilbraham's 1758 Militia Uniform:

Blue White-faced coats
Waistcoats of Buff Leather
Black Breeches and Gaiters
Black Tricorner Hats

The population grew rapidly:

1760 – 350
1765 - 491
1776 - 1,057
1790 - 1,555
1800 - 1,743

Lucinda Brewer married Zenas Crane, founder of Crane Paper Co. in Dalton, in 1809. Zenas was from eastern Massachusetts and selected Dalton in 1799 as the site of his mill due to the "inexhaustible" supply of pure drinking water. The mill was finished in 1801 and was know as the Old Berkshire. This mill was the nucleus of the Crane Paper Company which today is the sole supplier of paper for U.S. currency. Crane Park in Wilbraham is one of the pieces of land they owned.

A rattlesnake killed Lt. Thomas Mirick's son Timothy on August 6, 1761 south on Main Street below Rattlesnake Peak. This was about 900 feet south of Main Street on today's Oakland Street.

The Justices of the Peace in 1814 were Abel Bliss, Jr., Robert Sessions, Samuel F. Merrick, Augustus Sessions, and Walter Stebbins.

The first School Committee (5 people) was appointed in 1764. An average of $70 per year was appropriated over the next ten years for the schools in town.

438 Main Street in Hampden was called "The Fort." This was where the militia stored its ammunition in the time between 1792 - 1812. The Hampden (South Co.) militia trained during this same time period in front of the Mile Tree School with the Wilbraham Company.

Levi Bliss was the father of three of the children who died in the boating accident at Nine Mile Pond (2 sons, 1 daughter). Dr. Samuel F. Merrick had one daughter drown and Noah Warriner had one daughter drown. Lovely brownstone monuments in Adams Cemetery memorialize these unfortunate children.

David Bliss, who is buried in Adams Cemetery (10/5/1828 at 84) was originally from Longmeadow. His daughter Lydia was the first person buried in the burying ground in Hampden (June 1755).

C

www.ingramcontent.com/pod-product-compliance
Lightning Source LLC
LaVergne TN
LVHW050633100826

845148LV00011B/1852
9780788415418